THE
NEWFOUNDLAND
AND LABRADOR
COCKTAIL BOOK

THE NEWFOUNDLAND AND LABRADOR
COCKTAIL
BOOK

THE DEFINITIVE GUIDE TO COCKTAILS
ACROSS THE PROVINCE

PETER WILKINS

CO-FOUNDER OF THE NEWFOUNDLAND DISTILLERY COMPANY

BREAKWATER

Breakwater Books
P.O. Box 2188, St. John's, NL, Canada, A1C 6E6
www.breakwaterbooks.com

A CIP catalogue record for this book is available from Library and Archives Canada.

ISBN 9781550819489 (softcover)

We acknowledge the support of the Canada Council for the Arts.

We acknowledge the financial support of the Government of Canada through the Department of Heritage and the Government of Newfoundland and Labrador through the Department of Tourism, Culture, Arts and Recreation for our publishing activities.

Printed and bound in Canada.

Breakwater Books is committed to choosing papers and materials for our books that help to protect our environment. To this end, this book is printed on a recycled paper and other sources that are certified by the Forest Stewardship Council®.

 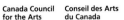

CONTENTS

FOREWORD

—— BY LISA MOORE ——

Peter Wilkins looks alarmed. I've tried to paraphrase something he's said.

So, I said, a cocktail is superior to a glass of beer and wine? His look says the interview is off the rails. He holds his palm up straight before me, as if to bring time itself to a halt.

No, no, he says. Beer and wine are very important.

Very important, I say.

They just come later in the evening, Peter says. Hopefully, in an evening of drinking there will be food. That's when we want the beer and wine. But a good cocktail comes at the beginning of the evening.

He has warmed to the subject.

A good cocktail kicks off the celebratory moment, he says. But beer and wine—

Beer and wine with food? I repeat. He looks reassured.

Yes, he says. We start with the cocktail, and there will be more cocktails in a perfect night of drinking. But beer and wine have their place.

Yes, of course, I say.

I am remembering a lot of beer and wine.

I am remembering the parties of the '90s. All the parties. Children with stacks of VHS movies, children jumping on the beds, boinging each other into the air.

Children came to the parties, grandparents were there too. People of all ages. Artists, writers, journalists, philosophy professors, students, musicians, lawyers, bus drivers. People who told stories, held the room, raucous laughter, and dancing. The parties moved from house to house in downtown St. John's. Any excuse for a party. Kitchens were jammed with people, and people spilled over into living rooms, hallways, staircases. Once Mark Ferguson's shoe was eventually discovered in the freezer of Medina Stacey's fridge, next to a chilling bottle of vodka. Someone had hidden Mark's shoe so he wouldn't be able to leave the party. The sun broke like an egg yolk all over Quidi Vidi Lake, and Mark hobbled away in one shoe. Someone ran out of the house with the other shoe held high, waving it back and forth, yelling, Here! Here's your shoe! The music still thumping through all the walls.

At Michelle and Peter's people could sleep over. The house on Monkstown Road: labyrinthine. Bedrooms opening onto bedrooms onto corridors, more bedrooms. Easy to get lost. All kinds of things kept opening up into other things, all night long.

Often there was drama, there were trysts, the kitchen swelled with people when the bars closed, the way the chambers of the heart fill with blood, people circulating through the rooms.

Michelle Mahoney says: Dancing of course, always dancing.

Jim Bradley demanded *Heart of Glass*. He smoked with a cigarette holder, talked of the Trinity and Whitehead and Henry James's *The Golden Bowl*; people argued about elections and oil and who would go on a beer run.

It was the kind of dancing where the floor bowed under the weight, where body parts inevitably bonked or rubbed or swivelled, where people held their beer over their heads and sometimes a rope of foam flung itself out the bottle and rained down on the person you were dancing with.

Voices rose and fell like crashing waves. In winter the children slept on the mounds of a second-hand mink with red satin lining, or something in leopard print. Michelle had beautiful clothes—antiques or brand new—dresses laid out on a chair, jewels on her bureau. People waited in the porch for taxis that never came. They tried to escape, but they were lured back onto the dance floor. And the food? The table was covered in smoked salmon, bowls of salsa, bruschetta, puff pastry stuffed with rich concoctions of mushroom and cognac, there were mussels and cheese with veins of mould and French bread, and don't pretend you weren't there. Don't pretend it wasn't you flirting with the new guy who was in town writing a novel, or the artist who was working with spray paint, or the actor who still wore the makeup from the show at the Hall. It was you who fell onto the oil executive's guitar and crunched it under your bony butt. We partied through the boom and bust, the rise and fall of fortune. The

digital age bolstered and betrayed, housing peaked, and all the old people who had lived downtown for generations were gentrified right out onto passing ice floes, back when there were still ice floes. On the rocks? It became a thing to put iceberg bits in your drinks. We partied through all of that.

Peter Wilkins has a British accent, and he wears bright paisley shirts that are crisp and stylish. When Michelle and Peter were flush, there was champagne. When they weren't flush, there was still beer and wine and martinis.

They'd met in a bar in Prague. Michelle had finished her master's in philosophy and headed off to travel, went into a place called Jo's Bar, run by two Canadians, and asked for a job. She didn't want to come back to Newfoundland, not yet. Can you cook? No. Can you tend bar? No. Can you wash dishes? She could wash dishes.

They'd shown her the dish pit and taken her out front to meet a few of the regulars, and there was Peter. Backgammon, Scrabble, other board games, expats from everywhere. The opening scene of their love story was a perpetual party. One day Michelle headed to a doctor and discovered she was five months' pregnant. A couple of years later, with a second child on the way, she asked Peter if he loved her. He said yes. And she said, Good, because we're going back to Newfoundland.

This is an introduction to a recipe book about cocktails, about community, about gatherings that only end at dawn; this is about breaching the inky dark and stepping out into amber light.

Obviously, this introduction is awash with nostalgia. I'm writing in the midst of a pandemic, during a lockdown, no parties, when people are told to keep to their "tight ten."

I am writing about a time before tight.

I am writing about loose, about youth, about corridors full of doors and you could choose any door, and beyond was another door. About going

through. And about love and friendship, because that's what happened at those parties.

The children set up a business at these parties, standing guard at the door of the bathroom, demanding admission. They made a mint. The talk was about art and business. Maybe even religion. I think people smoked inside. I think glasses were broken. I think we dressed up. I am pretty sure I wore a tiara to a few of these parties. I am pretty sure a dollar-store feather boa in fluorescent pink.

There were weddings and the bouquets were full of wildflowers, and the children of these unions climbed up onto the altar, toddlers in white stockings with frilly bottoms, climbing with lugubrious agility, and then dainty steps across the red carpet. Because the truth is most people had kids before they got married, and it was a mystery why anybody bothered with the ceremony, except for the party.

William Carter (left) and Peter Wilkins

I'm interviewing Peter in the Newfoundland Distillery in Clarke's Beach. Big windows, a view of the bay, a wood stove. An exceptional martini, Seaweed Gin, a velvet spritz of elation. Peter's business partner and the head distiller, Bill Carter, is there. They take me for a tour of the distillery. They use ingredients from the area for the particular taste of their gin—seaweed, berries, spruce.

And how do you not get drunk, I ask Peter.

Restraint and maturity, he says. There's a real danger that if you get drunk, you'll have to retire early and miss the party.

Maturity, because these parties have spanned almost four decades. Peter and Michelle moved to Clarke's Beach. The house had belonged to Michelle's grandparents; she spent part of her childhood there. It was another house with a lot of doors. Lots of rooms for guests to crash. But this house also has rolling lawns, a tree swing, a view of the ocean. Everyone makes the drive from St. John's. The dancing is outdoors.

Dancing always, Michelle says. Always.

Music blasting, a bonfire, the children are teenagers now. And now they are adults. And now they have left the province, or they have stayed. Marshmallows on long sticks, every face varnished in the flickering firelight.

The machines in the distillery look space age. They look like rockets with polished steel and copper, little portals to check how things are going inside. There are pipes and funnels, wheels and gadgets, everything gleaming. We can climb inside these machines and blast off, time travel. We can go forward or back. We can stay up all night.

Peter gives me a bottle of Seaweed Gin for later. We drive back to our home around the bay in a snowstorm. I plan to have a cocktail in my sister-in-law's hot tub. I will follow the martini recipe in this book. My sister-in-law and I get in the tub, and the roiling heat and jet streams pummel our bodies. The gin glass (Peter says a martini glass is nice, but use whatever you have, make do!) is covered in ice on the outside. Peter says not to pay any attention to 007's preference—*shaken not stirred*; that will just bruise the gin.

The wind and sleet trying to rip the features off my face. The ocean is just right there; we can hear it hammering.

The gin tastes like the snowsquall coming across the lawn, or the snowsquall tastes like the gin. It tastes like a party, or youth, or where we are now, in the celebratory moment. At the beginning of the party.

INTRODUCTION

MY LIFE WITH COCKTAILS

I still remember my first cocktail. It was amazing, immediately unveiling a whole new world to me. I sipped it slowly to make sure the flavours I was tasting were real, constant, and not some fleeting piece of magic. The experience was nothing less than idyllic. Warm, golden early evening sun, a garden full of fragrant flowers, and the excitement of a multi-generational party with family and friends. I was still a teen-ager, and my role was to make sure everyone had a drink, particularly a glass of Pimm's, which was being served from a jug into tall glasses with lots of ice and fruit—apples, raspberries, strawberries, as well as a slice of cucumber and a sprig of mint. Once the party was in full swing, my sister and I found ourselves with a glass each and felt obliged to give it a try. We both loved it. I was a believer.

I have had many favourites over the years. The amazing thing about cocktails is how you and they evolve over time. Every cocktail is instantly exciting—will it be as perfect as last time? Will it be the best one ever? Who am I sharing it with? What am I celebrating? In my book, the end of a busy day counts as celebration. And my cocktail almost always changes. The key is to try to fit the mood and the weather, and to use what you have on hand.

One of my all-time party favourites is the Lemon Drop (vodka, fresh lemon juice, and sugar), as a shot. It's easy to make and the perfect drink to help get the toe-tappers on the dance floor. It's light, elevating, and refreshing, and seems to put everyone in a great mood.

I suspect the cocktail bars I frequented in my youth were not as good as they seemed then. But there was nothing as exciting as meeting friends at a cocktail bar and ordering "jugs" to share our favourites, with everyone over-enthusiastically singing the praises of their own selections! There is never

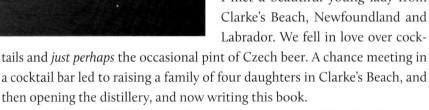

an outright winner, as subjectivity is what makes it such fun.

When you find a really good cocktail bar, over time you should work your way through their cocktail list. You get to know the bar staff and other customers, which is so much fun, especially when you're away from home. I've been to many, but one stands out—Jo's Bar in Prague. I was living and working in the stunning Czech capital—pretty much living the dream. One day at Jo's Bar I met a beautiful young lady from Clarke's Beach, Newfoundland and Labrador. We fell in love over cocktails and *just perhaps* the occasional pint of Czech beer. A chance meeting in a cocktail bar led to raising a family of four daughters in Clarke's Beach, and then opening the distillery, and now writing this book.

Cocktails—possibly life-changing and, most certainly, life-affirming!

WHEN TO DRINK COCKTAILS

I think of cocktails as a little celebration of the day, hour, company, a small feat, or a moment to savour. Cocktails at brunch, lunch, midafternoon, early evening, as an aperitif, a digestif, or late into the night—all are great ideas (but not on the same day).

As often as possible, but never quite often enough, I enjoy a big, proper lunch as my new kind of decadence. The best way to kick this off is a cocktail—of any kind. That said, the most common time I have a cocktail is at the end of the working day—safe in the knowledge that I've earned the evening to enjoy it. And my absolute favourite time is when friends or family come for dinner—the food is under control, and we toast their arrival with a cocktail! Sometimes we plan it in advance, and sometimes we ask them what they would like—as long as we are organized enough to have the necessary ingredients.

And while I love cocktails and am incessantly excited by them, there is always time for a glass of beer or wine too. Cocktails should be savoured, so if I am thirsty, beyond a glass of water, I might enjoy a bottle of beer—especially a local craft beer.

We usually have a glass of wine with dinner, as it goes better with food. It's such a thrill when you match the right wine to your food, and you can always revert to cocktails after dinner and continue to celebrate the day and each other.

SHARING COCKTAILS

After much compiling (the tough part) and testing (the fun part), I am presenting what I hope is the definitive guide to effortlessly making classic and contemporary cocktails using the best local ingredients from Newfoundland and Labrador. The key to a great cocktail is to remember that the whole process—from making it to sharing it to tasting it—is all about pleasure.

The cocktail recipes in this book are twists or slight refinements on many great and classic cocktails that have been enjoyed over the ages. Our sixty-nine cocktails are organized in categories, from "light" to those of a "certain delight," on to the more obvious "boozier," and, for something special, "the palate that is slightly choosier." These have been selected to showcase the full range and ensure there is a cocktail for everyone. You know what you like—you might want your cocktail to be made quickly, or to look beautiful, or, ideally, both., There is no definitive version of a cocktail, as they are all open to tweaks, additions, and subtractions. The key is to use the ingredients you have at hand in the purest, easiest, and most fun and enjoyable way possible. Ultimately, it is about lifting everyone's spirits (sorry, couldn't resist) to celebrate what are hopefully the best moments of your day.

This book also includes cocktails from 34 of the finest bars, breweries, and restaurants across the province—over 120 of them—from Clarke's Beach to St. John's, and from Labrador City to Corner Brook. Some of the most amiable and skilled bartenders from across the region graciously contributed their time—and their favourite cocktails—to this collection.

A LITTLE HISTORY OF THE NEWFOUNDLAND DISTILLERY

The Newfoundland Distillery Co. just sort of happened. My old friend William Carter, a cordon bleu chef, had cooked for a wide range of guests in Ottawa for over twenty years, including prime ministers and three American presidents. He'd returned to Newfoundland in 2016 and popped over one day to say hello.

It was a gorgeous summer day in late June, and we were sitting outside with a glass of white wine (not a cocktail, sorry!), and he announced that he wanted to make whisky and set up the first craft distillery in the province. My immediate reaction was "how cool is that?" Then it occurred to me that whisky takes at least three years to mature. I instantly suggested gin. Bill grinned and said he'd see me in a couple of weeks.

The gin was superb; we took it on tour and everyone agreed. Extraordinarily, everything fell into place, everyone was incredibly helpful, and by September we had federal and provincial permissions to distil. We then sourced equipment; by

January we were operating, and by May we had bottled our first full batch of vodka for sale at the Newfoundland Liquor Commission, soon followed by gin. We were in business. We are still scratching our heads.

Setting up a distillery hadn't been on my radar, but I appeared to be qualified. After all, I did have years of experience sampling cocktails and spirits, including a year travelling the world with one of my best friends, who was hired by a British TV company to investigate how other cultures approached alcohol. And Bill had often experimented with preserving fresh local produce in alcohol, so he knew how to produce and distil spirits. We became committed to celebrating the *terroir* of our province, using local ingredients and botanicals to make unique, interesting spirits that reflect where they come from—putting a little bit of the province in each bottle, celebrating the land and the sea. We have a Tasting Room, where we continue to concoct cocktails and showcase our spirits.

The Newfoundland Distillery is the first craft distillery in Newfoundland and Labrador. We use locally grown barley as the base spirit for many products, which include gins, rums, Aquavit, and vodkas. In 2020, much to Bill's delight, we began to lay down whisky.

Much to our delight and surprise, our spirits have won multiple awards:

- Best Varietal Vodka in Canada at the 2022 World Vodka Awards
- Double gold medal at the 2022 San Francisco World Spirits Awards for our Tom Collins Ready-to-Drink (RTD), gold medal for our Seaweed Gin and Vodka & Soda Tom Collins, and a silver medal for All N&L G&T RTD
- Best Canadian Contemporary Gin at the 2021 World Gin Awards for our Seaweed Gin
- Double gold from the 2018 San Francisco World Spirit Competition for our Seaweed Gin, and multiple silver medals for our Chaga Rum and Cloudberry Gin
- Silver medal with distinction from 2021 Canadian Artisan Spirit Competition for our Cloudberry Gin and a silver medal for our Seaweed Gin in 2018
- Best Spiced Rum in Canada from the World Rum Awards in 2019 for our Chaga Rum and for our Gunpowder & Rose Rum in 2020
- Gold medal at the 2020 New York Spirit Competition for our Seaweed Gin and a silver medal for our Cloudberry Gin
- Silver medal at the 2021 Rum Masters and at the 2021 San Francisco World Spirits Awards for our Gunpowder & Rose Rum
- Silver medal at the 2021 World Vodka Awards for our Rhubarb Vodka

Our Seaweed Gin is one of the best-selling gins in Newfoundland and Labrador, and our products are now available in Alberta, Nova Scotia, Ontario, Prince Edward Island, Quebec, and the United Kingdom. We are working on expanding to the rest of Canada and the United States, and then beyond.

OUR SPIRITS

AQUAVIT

Our Aquavit is the first spirit legally distilled in Newfoundland and Labrador to use grain grown here. The ingredients come from coast to coast—the Tuck's Bee Better Honey from Grand Falls-Windsor, the peat and juniper from Clarke's Beach, and a dash of savory from Mt. Scio Farm in St. John's. Aquavit is a Nordic spirit that is traditionally flavoured with local herbs and botanicals. We've made ours unique to Newfoundland, and in some ways it's a young "wan-nabe" whisky; there's a hint of smokiness from the campfire safely in the distance, a little bit of earthiness from the peat, herbal notes from the savory, and a comforting roundness from a small touch of honey. This is a young, smooth spirit, reminiscent of the aromas and purity of a walk through the Newfoundland wilderness. Aquavit can be enjoyed in many ways: straight, over ice, and in whisky-based cocktails; in an Old Fashioned, an Aquavit Sour, or even a hot toddy.

CHAGA RUM

Our Chaga Rum is a premium spirit made with five-year-old Demerara rum from Guyana, finely infused in Clarke's Beach with chaga mushrooms harvested from central Newfoundland and honey from Grand Falls-Windsor. The flavours capture the deep earthy notes of the chaga, which bring out rich hints of truffle, chocolate, and coffee, balanced by the classic deep notes of the rum, held together by a touch of honey—perfect for savouring and warming yourself up!

GUNPOWDER & ROSE RUM

Gunpowder & Rose Rum is made with the key elements of gunpowder, using  sea salt from the Newfoundland Salt Company for the taste of saltpetre (potassium nitrate); locally harvested kelp, which is a natural source of sulphur; and charred birch for the carbon flavour—all to contrast with the floral notes of wild roses. This makes for a unique aged rum that opens up with a gentle blast of gunpowder before the mellower tones come into play, with hints of vanilla followed by the aromatic rose scents. In the navy, rum was always "proofed" before the sailors were given their daily ration. The purser would put gunpowder in the rum and light it. If it flared up, the sailors would know they were getting their proper measure. Ours too has a little zing, but we've balanced it with a hint of roses to make an amber rum that satisfies those looking for a traditional rum and those seeking more subtle flavours with complex undertones.

CLOUDBERRY GIN

This gin is full of juniper and cloudberry (bakeapple) picked from the wilds of Placentia Bay, with a little savory from Mt. Scio Farm. We've tried to keep it pure and simple, using only local botanicals. This one is a little fruity, the cloudberries giving it a few citrus notes, which balance out the juniper.

SEAWEED GIN

Our Seaweed Gin is made using seaweed (dulse) harvested from the Grand Banks. Slightly salty, full of juniper, it makes you think you're in an ocean mist next to an herb garden. It is the savoury (flavour, not herb) companion to our Cloudberry Gin.

VODKA

Our Vodka is made with locally grown barley. It has a very subtle barley flavour and is incredibly smooth, with hints of vanilla and butter. We like to think it can win many "taste-offs" but do appreciate we might not be the most objective judges!

RHUBARB FLAVOURED VODKA

Rhubarb Flavoured Vodka is made with local rhubarb and partridgeberries (ling-onberries). It has the freshness and bite of just-picked rhubarb,

which is tempered with a dash of Tuck's Bee Better Honey from Grand Falls-Windsor. The base vodka's barley helps ensure a brilliantly rounded flavour. Lovely to drink on its own or as a flavourful twist in vodka-based cocktails, especially those with citrus. It also makes a fine martini.

OUR HANDCRAFTED BITTERS

CHAGA & CHANTERELLE BITTERS

Chaga & Chanterelle Bitters evoke the scent of summer with rich, woodsy flavours—a pure example of Newfoundland terroir. These are great for classic whisky- and rum-based cocktails.

CLASSIC BITTERS

Our Classic Bitters have all the hallmarks of the best-known bitters, with local botanicals added, such as alder pepper, sweet gale, and beet juice, along with the more traditional spices and herbs.

CLOUDBERRY BITTERS

Cloudberry capture the essence of bakeapples (cloudberries), with hints

of citrus and the barrens for a strong sense of Newfoundland terroir. Ideal for gin- and vodka-based cocktails.

SEAWEED & NETTLE BITTERS

Seaweed & Nettle Bitters' savoury notes of seaweed meld with a hint of salt and a little bite of nettle that announce Newfoundland terroir. Perfect for classic gin- and vodka-based cocktails.

SWEET GALE & WILD ROSE BITTERS

Sweet Gale & Wild Rose Bitters' aromatic flavours of sweet gale and floral notes of wild roses are pure representation of Newfoundland terroir. What could be better for classic gin- and vodka-based cocktails?

BUILDING YOUR COCKTAIL BAR

The one most important item for your cocktail bar is a bottle of your favourite spirit. I would probably choose Seaweed Gin—but then I would worry about my other favourites! Start with your favourites and keep adding. This cocktail book uses our spirits as the base for each drink, so we start with gins, vodkas, rums, and our Aquavit, which becomes our whisky ingredient in cocktails.

Then decide on the cocktail you would like to make. All cocktails have at least a sprinkle of something added to them to bring out the flavours of the spirit and make some magic in your glass. This varies from vermouths to liqueurs, bitters, citrus fruit, and a sweetener such as a liqueur or syrup. We've ensured that our spirits are featured here several times and that all the other bottles—bitters, vermouths, liqueurs, etc.—are used at least three times, to make your purchases worthwhile.

VERMOUTHS

You will be all set with a dry and a sweet vermouth—ideally, the best you can get!

LIQUEURS

A great starting point is an orange liqueur—Triple Sec, Cointreau, or Grand Marnier. A peach liqueur made in Ontario would be excellent. And maybe an elderflower liqueur too. Those are the key ones we use, and there are plenty more wonderful ones that are fun to play with.

ITALIAN BITTERS

The two best-known classic Italian aperitif bitters are Campari and Aperol. I tend to prefer Campari because the flavours suit me better and I like the colour. That said, most people in my house much prefer Aperol, so apparently there is no right or wrong.

FLAVOURING BITTERS

Flavouring bitters are small bottles of intensely flavoured bitters that you cannot drink on their own and that act as the seasoning of many superb cocktails. There are many bitters out there that are good fun to try. All great cocktail makers use bitters as all great cooks use herbs and spices—they either become the glue that combines the flavours and holds the drink together, or that extra little "pop" that makes the drink sing. In preparing your bar, choose one aperitif bitters and one or two of the others.

CITRUS FRUITS

Lemons and limes are in a surprising number of cocktails. That citrus kick, with a healthy dose of vitamin C, balanced by a little sweetness and mixed with a spirit, has been wooing people for centuries. Citrus can also be used as a garnish—it makes drinks look so much more inviting, and you can do many clever things with a simple peeler. The natural oils and zest of the citrus skins are amazing things, full of lightness and lift, and they give the cocktail that little bit of extra.

OTHER GARNISHES

Other great garnishes to have on hand, if you like martinis, are the best olives you can find and, for Manhattans (or our versions of them) and a surprising number of other cocktails, a jar of the finest maraschino cherries available.

SWEETENERS

Sometimes you can use a liqueur, which is full of sugars, to give your cocktail the necessary sweetness, but most often you will need extra help from a simple syrup. There are all sorts of variations that are pleasing enhancements, but the basic, classic simple syrup is just that—very simple to make.

SIMPLE SYRUP

Place equal amounts of sugar and water in a saucepan. Heat, stirring occasionally, until the sugar melts. Let cool and pour into a bottle or storage container. It will keep, covered, in the fridge for one to two weeks.

HONEY SIMPLE SYRUP

Instead of sugar, use honey. Proportions and method are the same as for simple syrup. Of course, the type of honey you use will affect the flavour. Lighter honeys, such as clover, will lift lighter cocktails up while the darker, stronger honeys are better for the darker spirits. Bees Knees and Gold Rush cocktails really benefit from honey simple syrup.

MAPLE SIMPLE SYRUP

This is rather key in the Maple Old Fashioned! Make it the same way as the other syrups, except with maple as the sweetener.

ROSE-PETAL-INFUSED SIMPLE SYRUP

This is the floral version and very versatile. If you don't have fresh rose petals, dried ones are fine, but ensure they are "food grade" petals. Health-food shops have them.

½ cup	sugar
½ cup	water
1	fresh rose or ¼ cup dried rose petals

If using a fresh rose, remove all the petals and discard remainder. Put petals, sugar, and water in saucepan. Heat, stirring occasionally, until sugar has dissolved. Allow to cool.

VANILLA SIMPLE SYRUP

Vanilla simple syrup can be added to lots of cocktails and is particularly good in those based on rum and whisky, where the vanilla notes gently enhance existing flavours. Use real vanilla extract; vanilla pods are even better.

½ cup	sugar
½ cup	water
1 tsp	pure vanilla extract or 1 vanilla pod

Combine sugar, water, and vanilla in saucepan. If using pod, cut it in half, lengthways, to help release the flavours. Heat, stirring occasionally, until sugar has dissolved. Allow to cool. Remove pod.

MOLASSES SIMPLE SYRUP

This name is a little misleading as it's not quite so simple. This is the best syrup for an Otterbury Fashioned; it makes the drink that much deeper and richer.

½ cup	fancy molasses
½ cup	water
1	cinnamon stick
2	cloves
pinch	allspice

Pour molasses and water into saucepan. Add spices. Heat, stirring occasionally, until molasses has dissolved and is fully integrated. Allow to cool. Remove cloves and cinnamon stick.

FRUIT AND HERB SIMPLE SYRUPS

We haven't called for many in this cocktail book. Where they are mentioned, you can just use the straight simple syrup, but if you do have the time, they are great enhancements. Try strawberry simple syrup for the Summer Kiss, blueberry simple syrup for the Blueberry Lemonade, raspberry simple syrup for the Cracklin' Rose, or rosemary simple syrup for your Tom Collins. Follow the simple syrup recipe and use a little less sugar, since you will get the extra sweetness from the fruit. Add ½ cup of fruit or ¼ cup of herbs to the saucepan as you start warming the water and sugar. Strain the simple syrup and do not force the extra bits of fruit through the strainer, as that will make the syrup cloudy.

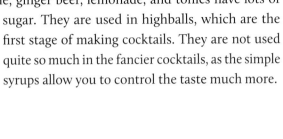

Drinks like cola, ginger ale, ginger beer, lemonade, and tonics have lots of sugar. They are used in highballs, which are the first stage of making cocktails. They are not used quite so much in the fancier cocktails, as the simple syrups allow you to control the taste much more.

COCKTAIL ESSENTIALS

SHAKERS

If you don't have a proper shaker, a Mason jar, jam jar, or any wide-mouthed bottle will do the trick. But if you want the best tool, our favourite is the two-part Boston Shaker used with a strainer. You make your drink in the bigger, bottom part that you can use to stir drinks too. There are other fine cocktail shakers—many people like the Cobbler, which has a top, a bottom, and a little lid you can lift off to strain directly from the shaker. But when you shake a cocktail, you create a bit of a vacuum and so it can become incredibly hard to open. While making Lemon Drops, I once wrecked a beautiful silver cocktail shaker by trying to open it with flat screwdrivers. Luckily, the hosts were incredibly gracious about their destroyed Cobbler.

STRAINERS

Our favourite strainer, with its useful spring to help control pouring, is technically called a Hawthorne strainer. Although we don't use others, a julep strainer and a V-shaped sieve are also great for straining drinks. If you don't have a strainer, a lid, spoon, colander, or sieve will do the trick. Failing that, you can use your (clean) fingers.

JIGGERS

Jiggers make the measuring easier. Most have multiple measurements so you can easily mix the perfect proportions for all your cocktails. If you don't have one, a screwtop bottle cap will do—just make sure you get the proportions right. That said, ultimately you can always eyeball it—I often do when making drinks I know well. Eyeballing is for home cocktails only, as it will break all the rules of legal bartending.

BAR SPOONS

Bar spoons have extended super-long handles so you can mix the full drink without getting your hands even close to the drink. They also usually have a corkscrew shape, which is oddly satisfying when you're stirring, although you shouldn't gaze too long, as you might overdo it. Bar spoons are slightly easier to use to make layered drinks such as the New York Sour. If you haven't got a proper bar spoon, any long-handled spoon should do the trick. Narrow is best so you can gently stir the spirits around the ice.

MUDDLERS

Muddlers are long wooden pestles used to break down fruit and herbs at the bottom of the glass so their flavours are more readily imparted into the cocktail. You can also chop the fruit or herbs with a knife, then put them in the glass and crush them a bit more with the back of a spoon.

CITRUS JUICERS

Lemons and limes (and even oranges and grapefruits) are always best freshly squeezed—it really does make all the difference in flavour. Citrus juicers are easy to find and use. If you don't have one, just cut the fruit into quarters and squeeze as hard as you can over the glass or into the shaker. If you are working at a bar or big party, you will need an electric juicer.

PEELERS

With a peeler, you can make pretty garnishes easily. You can also peel the citrus skin from the pith—the skin is where the natural oils are. Release them into the glass with a little squeeze, or even singe the peel with a match, then use as a garnish. If you don't have one, you must be proficient with a knife.

CHANNEL KNIVES

Channel knives' key utility is to make lovely, swirly citrus garnishes. You can peel long, thin strips and look incredibly professional. They also work as zesters.

COCKTAIL STICKS

Cocktail sticks really aren't essential, but they do make the olives, cherries, and garnishes look a lot more impressive. You can now get fancy reusable copper, silver, and stainless-steel ones and feel very smart. Failing that, a toothpick will do the job—or drop the olive or cherry into the bottom of the glass as a prize for finishing it!

Those people who take ice very, very seriously are quite right to do so. That said, circumstances can change your view on ice quickly, and sometimes you'll use whatever you can get.

It really is best if you can chill most, if not all, cocktails and you want good, big cubes of ice—not small bitty or holey ones that melt and turn your lovely cocktail into sad slush. You need good-sized ice trays (unless you have a bar or restaurant where you need an ice machine) that make one- to one-and-a-half-inch cubes. If you are fancy and like what I would call alcohol-forward drinks, like Negronis, it would be good to have a giant two-inch square or sphere (my fav) ice cube. They're easy to find and fun to play with.

Some people love clear ice, but I am quite happy seeing a bit of frosted white in my ice cubes. If you want to make the perfect ice, fill your tray with hot water and freeze it. (I've never believed in drinking warm or hot water from a tap, but that might be a European thing, as no one else seems to mind.). Better still, fill up the bottom of a cooler with water to about two inches and then pop the whole thing in the freezer. You'll have a clear block and you can also put in ice trays.

Perhaps the greatest is iceberg ice. It just doesn't melt; it's so compacted and old (10,000 years plus) that it will last forever in your drink. You do,

however, need to know someone who can get the iceberg ice safely for you and then find a proper ice-cutting kit. It is well worth the effort.

GLASSES

So much fun can be had with glasses. If you are lucky enough to have a range of fancy glasses, from super-smart hip and trendy ones to eclectic bric-a-brac selections (which might be even trendier: I can't keep up), cocktails are the best and most fun way to use them. But any glass, or even a jam jar, Mason jar, or mug will do the trick. Having a cocktail is fun, and there should be no stress! In fact, the glassware suggestions below aren't always the ones featured in the photos: it's fun to change it up.

Typically, everyone uses a particular shape of glass to help enhance the pleasures of the cocktail—the wide brim of a martini glass gives greater surface area for the gin to be exposed to the air, which opens the drink up, revealing its complexities and flavours. It is also easy to pop an olive on a cocktail stick in there without losing them. And the long stem helps to keep the drink cool, in the hope that the drinker won't warm the spirits up with their hand. The tall Collins glass holds a good amount of ice, spirits, fizz, and anything else, for a long refreshing drink. A rocks glass is the classic tumbler-style glass and very versatile. Ideal for a short, strong drink over ice or one with some mix, like a gin and tonic.

Keep your glasses chilled in the fridge, if possible—especially your martini glasses.

TECHNIQUES

Sometimes we can get a little overexcited with all of the accoutrements and forget we just need to pour the drink! Other times it's essential to learn other techniques.

SHAKING

Some drinks really do have to be shaken to both mix them and cool them, so they will be the right temperature. Very boozy drinks, like the martini and Manhattan, should just be stirred, as apparently you might "bruise the booze." You aren't going to hurt it, but you can overdo it.

Put the ingredients in your shaker over ice and give it a shake for around fifteen seconds. If you have very small ice cubes, you should do a little less (otherwise it will be too diluted), and if you have big ones, keep going for another three to five seconds. The art of shaking is to use a bit of rhythm; try not to put your hands all over it, as they will warm the shaker. The pros

like to hold it a bit like a football, end to end. Get into your rhythm and give it a go. Then strain and pour.

A dry shake is when you are shaking without ice, like when you're using egg whites and need to get the emulsification going to thicken the drink and create foam. Shaking it with ice makes your work harder, and it takes a lot longer to make your drink. You can tell quite easily when the drink has thickened; it just feels more solid. Stop, pop some ice in, give another quick shake to cool it, then strain and pour.

STRAINING

This isn't as hard as it sounds. With a Hawthorne strainer to keep the ice behind, pour the cooled cocktail gently into the glass. If you are making more complicated cocktails where you have fruit or herbs that you only want as a flavouring and not in the glass, you can "fine strain" your cocktail (a step I try to avoid).

GARNISHING

The easiest way to garnish is to add an olive or maraschino cherry: you can pop it on a cocktail stick. Or, use a thin half-slice of lime or lemon, or a quarter-slice of orange or grapefruit. And if you like perching your citrus fruit, just cut a small nick in the middle of the fruit and place on the side of the glass.

For stronger drinks, a little bit of peel, gently singed to release the oils, is the best way to go.

THE NEWFOUNDLAND DISTILLERY COCKTAILS

HIGHBALLS

Gin and Tonic (G&T)

Newfoundland and
Labrador G&T

Rum and Cola

Dark and Stormy

Moscow Mule

Vodka Soda

SWEET

Conception Bay Bellini

Strawberry Daiquiri

Strawberry Fields

Cloudberry Orangesicle

Sex on Clarke's Beach

Woo Woo

Sea Breeze

Cosmopolitan

The Layla

LIGHT

Summer Kiss

Blueberry Lemonade

Gin Fizz

Chambord Gin Fizz

Tom Collins

Rhubarb Refresher

Cuba Libre

Gin Basil Smash

Dirty Mojito

Cracklin' Rose

Lemon Drop

Cherry Jane's Last Dance

A CERTAIN DELIGHT

Clover Club

Periscope

The Goldrush

Aquavit Sour

Thyme on Our Side

Paper Plane

A Boy Named Sue

Bees Knees

Red Sky at Night

The In-Cloud

Bell Island Iced Tea

BOLDER

Cable Car

Salty Sailor

Harvest Moon

Espresso Martini

Honeysuckle

Man O' War

Hallo Spaceboy

BOOZIER

Classic Martini

Bitter, Sweet, and Twisted

Bronx

Manhattan

Rumhattan

High Horse

Otterbury Fashioned

Maple Rum Old Fashioned

Classic Daiquiri

Atlantic 75

Seaweed Margarita

FOR THE PALATE THAT'S CHOOSIER

Caesar

'Til the Bitter End

New York Sour

Negroni

Boulevardier

Newfoundland Negroni

Tarnished Nail

Eggnog (for two)

London Calling

White Lady

Fiddler's Green

Canadiano

Last Word

THE NEWFOUNDLAND DISTILLERY Co

GUNPOWDER & ROSE RUM

JAMAICAN RUM, WILD NEWFOUNDLAND RO
WITH KELP, CHARRED BIRCH & SEA SALT
FOR GUNPOWDER FLAVOURS.

Spiced Rum / Rhum Épicé
Infused in Clarke's Beach, Newfoundland

alc./vol   750

HIGHBALLS

I s a Gin and Tonic a cocktail? A Rum and Coke? Technically, they're considered "highball cocktails." If this really *is* your introduction to cocktail making, this is the easiest way to become an expert.

The glass is generally tall and thin, hence the "high" part of the highball, but you can easily use a good-sized tumbler. Highballs are typically long drinks with a single spirit base and a long, fizzy, usually sweetened mix, and a single garnish, typically citrus.

We will present six highball classics and then cover a range of alternatives you can make in an instant. Highballs should be a guaranteed result and very quick and easy! Remember: plenty of ice, great spirits, and the best mixes you can get your hands on—all mixed to the right proportions.

GIN AND TONIC (G&T)

This is the classic highball cocktail—and so internationally famous that it is has probably single-handedly led to the global boom in craft gin. Each gin producer has their own hallmark recipe—adding things like cucumbers, grapefruits, and rowanberries to showcase their gin. Using the best tonic available allows the gin to flourish and shine—along with a slice of lime or lemon.

In the nineteenth century, tonics were often consumed as medicines—most notably in India, where the British made their soldiers drink tonic with

quinine as an antidote to malaria. The soldiers, not surprisingly, disliked drinking it, since it was truly disgusting. The only way they could be persuaded was to mix it with gin. And that was the origin of what became known as a G&T.

Nowadays, there are lots of flavours of high-end tonics, such as elderflower and Mediterranean. Better tonics have a more complex range of botanicals in their ingredients, including cinchona bark—the natural source of quinine. Crucially, they are lot less sweet and use real cane sugar, rather than glucose-fructose, which is a significant improvement.

Through hard work and experimentation, I have created a few of my favourites. Everyone's palate is different, so you should commit yourself to rigorous tasting of flavour combinations to discover your favourites. Some people love adding half an ounce of fresh lime juice, which is delicious, but I prefer mine the straightforward, no-messing-with-it way!

1 ½ oz   Seaweed Gin or Cloudberry Gin
            (or other)
2 ½ oz   high-quality tonic
            lime slice (lemon or orange,
                if preferred), for garnish

Glass: *rocks or a tall Collins*

Place ice in your glass. Pour in gin and then tonic. Stir well to cool. Add citrus slice. Enjoy.

NEWFOUNDLAND AND LABRADOR G&T

This is the "all Newfoundland and Labrador" G&T using the superb Third Place Tonic from the Third Place Cocktail Company, based in St. John's, mixed with our Cloudberry Gin. This is so good we put it in a can!

Technically, this is as about as complex as it gets in a highball cocktail as their tonic is concentrated. It is fantastic that the tonic, like our spirits, is handmade in small batches. Company founders Dan and Kris use the finest ingredients with traditional flavours, so the tonic has much less sugar than others, which allows all the other classic tonic flavours to come through.

1 ½ oz   Cloudberry Gin
½ oz   Third Place Tonic
2 ½ oz   club soda
       lime slice, for garnish

Glass: *rocks or a tall Collins*

Place ice in your glass. Pour in gin and then tonic. Add club soda and stir well to cool. Garnish and enjoy.

RUM AND COLA

This, without doubt, is the highball of Newfoundland, the one everyone has. The biggest debate here is whether you like Coke or Pepsi. I wasn't a great fan of Rum and Cola until we came out with our Gunpowder & Rose Rum. Now it's one of my absolute favourites, with a good squeeze of lime that lightens the sweetness of the cola. Everyone knows exactly how much rum they like and whether they just want the cola to colour the rum or whether the rum should be swimming in it! As with all cocktails, it's imperative you enjoy it your way.

1 ½ oz   Gunpowder & Rose Rum
2 ½ oz   cola
          lime slice, for garnish

Glass: rocks or a tall Collins

Place ice in your glass. Pour in rum and then cola. Stir well to cool. Garnish with lime. Enjoy.

DARK AND STORMY

I wonder if this cocktail was named for Newfoundland weather…But what could be more pleasurable than to sip a Dark and Stormy next to the fire, looking out at the big dark clouds with wild winds and rain lashing about! This classic, ubiquitous cocktail delivers what it promises, a hint of rum, the zip of a good ginger beer, and a hint of fresh lime. It is always refreshing and a good go-to when you're unsure of what to have.

1 ½ oz	Gunpowder & Rose Rum
3 oz	ginger beer
½ oz	freshly squeezed lime juice
	lime slice, for garnish

Glass: rocks or a tall Collins

Place ice in your glass. Pour in rum and then ginger beer. Add lime juice. Stir well, to cool. Add lime. Enjoy.

MOSCOW MULE

Apparently, the Moscow Mule came about in Los Angeles when the new owner of a vodka brand and the owner of a pub with too much ginger beer in stock decided to mix the two. As the tale goes, one of them had a girl-friend with a copper factory making copper mugs, so the vodka owner, a smart marketer, visited all the bars in the city to take photos of their drink served in copper mugs.

The key is to use a proper ginger beer that gives the drink a bit of spice along with the vodka and lime. While a copper mug actually keeps it properly cold—which is perfect on those hot sunny days—I usually have mine in a tall Collins glass. I could be tempted, however, if I did have a proper copper mug, not a stainless-steel one lined with copper.

1 ½ oz	vodka
3 oz	ginger beer
½ oz	freshly squeezed lime juice
	lime slice, for garnish

Glass: *rocks or a tall Collins*

Place ice in your glass. Pour in vodka and then ginger beer. Add lime juice. Stir well to cool. Add garnish. Enjoy.

VODKA SODA

This is the purists' drink and especially good if you're watching your calories, even if vodka is a fermented, then distilled grain, with the sugars turning into alcohol. It tastes light and refreshing and so tasty with bitters and a squeeze of any citrus fruit. You can also pop fresh herbs in, such as rosemary, mint, and thyme. (We also liked this one so much we put it in a can.)

1 ½ oz	vodka
3 oz	soda
2–3	dashes of Classic Bitters
	lime slice (or any citrus fruit you fancy), for garnish

Glass: *rocks or a tall Collins*

Place ice in your glass. Pour in vodka and then soda. Stir well to cool. Add lime. Enjoy.

EXTRA HIGHBALLS

———

Once you've perfected the art of the basic highball, you can go wild, starting with variations such as Aquavit and soda, Aquavit and ginger ale, Gunpowder & Rose Rum and ginger ale, and vodka and tonic.

SWEET

This is the title we've always used for this collection of drinks in the Tasting Room. While it is largely correct, it's also partially a misnomer—the drinks aren't overly sweet, but they are certainly not bitter. And neither do they require palates accustomed to all kinds of cocktails. These are just a little bit sweeter and veer toward the sugary side, rather than the boozy or citrus side.

Suffice to say, these are the easy-drinking cocktails that everyone loves—a great way to get your Great-Aunt Betty involved in the celebrations.

CONCEPTION BAY BELLINI

The Bellini started at the super-hip Harry's Bar in Venice during the 1950s in the glory days of Italian cinema and style. A small bar just off the Grand Canal, Harry's is now so famous it's hard to get in. Their cocktails are fabulous.

The Bellini typically was made with fresh peach purée and topped up with Prosecco, which is produced in the foothills around Venice. We love the lightness of the original Bellini but have always been a bit short on fresh peaches, so we opt for vodka and, ideally, Dillon's Peach Schnapps from Ontario, where peaches are abundant. We add a bit of fresh lemon and simple syrup to give it a bit of fruitiness and sweetness.

It is a classic summer drink. Who needs the Grand Canal when you've got Conception Bay?

1 oz	vodka
½ oz	peach schnapps
½ oz	simple syrup
½ oz	freshly squeezed lemon juice
2–3 oz	sparkling wine (Benjamin Bridge or other)
	orange peel strip, for garnish

Glass: *stemmed wineglass*

Put ice in your cocktail shaker. Pour vodka over the ice. Add schnapps, syrup, and juice. Shake well for no more than 10 seconds so it doesn't water down, and strain into a glass. Top with sparkling wine. Stir gently, garnish, and enjoy.

STRAWBERRY DAIQUIRI

If the full-on daiquiri is too intense for you, this just might be the introduction you need to the glorious world of daiquiris. It has all the hallmarks of the proper daiquiri—rum, fresh lime juice, and simple syrup—with muddled strawberries to make it a little sweeter and fruitier. Because the flavours are so concentrated, club soda makes it a longer drink. Glorious.

1–2	strawberries
2 oz	Gunpowder & Rose Rum
½ oz	simple syrup
½ oz	freshly squeezed lime juice
1 oz	club soda
	lime slice, for garnish

Glass: *tumbler*

Roughly chop strawberries. Muddle them in a cocktail shaker. Put in ice. Pour in rum, add syrup and juice, shake until chilled. Strain mix into tumbler filled with crushed ice or ice cubes. Top with club soda and garnish. Enjoy.

STRAWBERRY FIELDS

———

And yes, Strawberry Fields should always be forever! This is a rich, delightful drink. The liqueur works as a strong base for the citrus and sugar mix, which is enhanced with muddled strawberries. This is all held together by the shaken egg whites, which emulsify and thicken the drink to create something rather special.

It's easy to buy a carton of pasteurized egg whites, if you prefer not to separate your eggs. If you do separate the eggs, you can always make hollandaise sauce with your egg yolks.

1–2	strawberries
1 ½ oz	Cloudberry Gin
1 oz	Elderflower Liqueur
½ oz	simple syrup
¾ oz	egg whites
½ oz	freshly squeezed lemon juice
1 oz	club soda
	strawberry, for garnish

Glass: *coupe or flute*

Use pre-chilled glass or put ice cubes in glass to chill it. Roughly chop strawberries, place in a cocktail shaker, and muddle. Put ice in your cocktail shaker. Pour in gin. Add liqueur, syrup, egg whites, and lemon juice to the shaker. Shake well, no more than 10 seconds. Empty ice from your glass and strain your mix into it. Garnish and enjoy.

CLOUDBERRY ORANGESICLE

This really does taste the like the old-school *orangesicle* ice cream, and perhaps is the grown-up version of it—the citrus of the gin blending with the orange flavour. A treat indeed, and surprisingly easy to make!

1 ½ oz	Cloudberry Gin
½ oz	orange liqueur
⅓ oz	vanilla syrup
⅓ oz	freshly squeezed lemon juice
¾ oz	freshly squeezed orange juice
1 oz	egg white
	orange slice, for garnish

Glass: *tall Collins*

Put all ingredients in your cocktail shaker. Dry shake (without ice) for 15 to 20 seconds. Add ice and shake again until chilled. Strain into a tall glass with ice and garnish. Enjoy.

SEX ON CLARKE'S BEACH

———

Everyone has made lots of jokes about this, most of them not very good. We are on Conception Bay, after all.

Adding peach schnapps to the vodka gives it a bit of body, sweetness, and flavour. Sex on the Beach (maybe not ours) was a very popular cocktail in the 1980s and 1990s. Then everyone seemed to take their cocktails a bit too seriously, so now this one is mostly confined to tropical holidays. It's still a great and very smooth cocktail that is super easy to make. So have a go and see how bad *your* jokes are.

1 oz	vodka
1 oz	peach schnapps
½ oz	freshly squeezed lemon juice
1 ½ oz	cranberry juice
1 ½ oz	orange juice
	maraschino cherry, for garnish

Glass: *tall*

Put all ingredients in an ice-filled cocktail shaker. Shake until chilled. Fill glass with ice and strain mix into it. Garnish and enjoy.

WOO WOO

Who doesn't want to go Woo Woo? It's closely related to Sex on Clarke's Beach, simply without the orange juice and with more cranberry juice. In many ways it can be considered the fancy version of the vodka and cranberry highball that many people love. The schnapps helps sweeten the cranberry juice to make this a very easy-drinking and refreshing cocktail.

It's also easy to turn into a shot with just 1 oz vodka, ½ oz schnapps, and ½ oz cranberry juice. It is much lighter than other shots and isn't going to make you wonder why you drank it.

2 oz	vodka
1 oz	peach schnapps
3 oz	cranberry juice
	lime slice, for garnish

Glass: *rocks or a tall Collins*

Fill your cocktail shaker with ice. Add all your ingredients and shake well until chilled—no more than 10 seconds. Fill glass with ice and strain mix into it. Garnish and enjoy.

SEA BREEZE

This is the final of the trio of 1980s and 1990s easy-drinking, slightly fruity cocktails. Note how they all fit together for a beautiful sunset on Conception Bay.

I drank quite a few of these in Prague back in the 1990s. I considered it my healthy drink because of the vitamin C from the grapefruit juice. I loved the bitterness of the grapefruit, slightly sweetened by the cranberry juice. I was lucky to know a few bartenders who would always over pour, which was permissible back then.

2 oz	vodka
3 ½ oz	grapefruit juice
½ oz	cranberry juice

Glass: *tall Collins*

Fill your glass with ice (no need for a cocktail shaker for this one). Pour the vodka over, add grapefruit juice, and give it a stir to mix and chill. Top with cranberry juice. Enjoy.

COSMOPOLITAN

This one broke out as Carrie's favourite tipple in the *Sex in the City* television series, which was set in New York. The show started in the 1990s and has just been revived (again), possibly bringing the cosmo back into fashion. Perhaps it never fell out?

This is a light, refreshing cocktail that continues the run of cranberry juice as an ingredient. This time it is also the blending of vodka with the orange liqueur and lime that gives it the needed balance and hint of complexity and mystery. This is a modern cocktail for everyone—not just television stars. You can dream of glitzy New York—or the joys of a calm, cool bay.

1 oz	vodka
1 oz	Triple Sec
½ oz	freshly squeezed lemon juice
1 ½ oz	cranberry juice
	lime slice, for garnish

Glass: *chilled martini*

Put ice in your martini glass, if it isn't already chilled. Fill your cocktail shaker with ice. Add all your ingredients to the shaker and shake well until chilled, but no more than 10 seconds. Empty your cocktail glass and strain mix into it. Garnish and enjoy.

THE LAYLA

This is another of those cocktails that brings back memories from my youth—it's not quite like the orangesicle, but the egg white and jam make it a little more special than a straight cocktail. If you don't have strawberry rhubarb jam, one or the other will do. We're very lucky to have superb locally made jams; they really do make the difference.

The Layla is like a grown-up fruit shake that feels a little more fun and is definitely a little more decadent.

1–2	strawberries
1 ½ oz	Rhubarb Vodka
1 ½ tsp	strawberry-rhubarb jam
½ oz	simple syrup
½ oz	lemon juice
½ oz	egg white
	strawberry, for garnish

Glass: *tall Collins*

Roughly chop strawberries. Muddle them in a cocktail shaker. Add all other ingredients. Give the Layla a good dry shake (without ice) for 15 to 20 seconds to combine all ingredients, especially the jam, and let it emulsify with the egg white. Add ice to your cocktail shaker and shake again to chill. Strain mix into tall glass with ice. Garnish and enjoy.

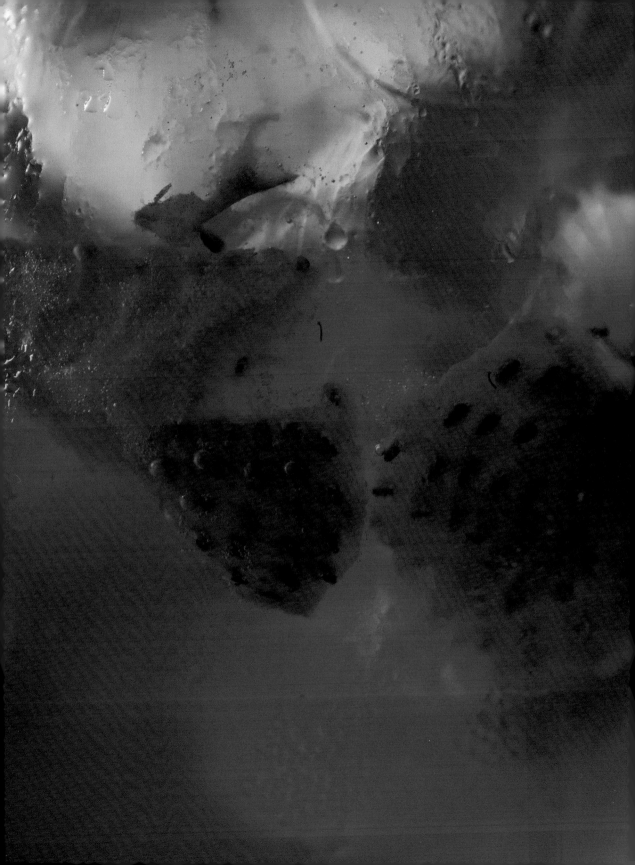

LIGHT

As the name suggests, these are all light cocktails—long, refreshing, and usually with fruit added. These are the crowd-pleasers, as there's nothing too radical or strange going on, just an idyllically composed drink to help you celebrate the day, evening, or night.

SUMMER KISS

Let's dream of summer kisses and a little bit of summer loving all year long. This is a superbly refreshing drink at any time of the year, but it's best with fresh strawberries from the garden. The drink is based on the classic mix of spirit, sugar, and citrus, with strawberries added. And it looks beautiful in the glass, the bright green of the mint leaf contrasting with the drink's deep pink. This is another one of our cocktails that is so good we've put it in a can.

1 ½ oz	Rhubarb Vodka
½ oz	simple syrup
½ oz	freshly squeezed lemon juice
1 tbsp	(heaping) chopped strawberries
2 oz	club soda
	strawberry, for garnish

Glass: *good-size rocks or Collins*

Put chopped strawberries in a tumbler and muddle. If the mood is right, pour in a splash of vodka to help with the muddling. Fill tumbler with ice. Pour in remaining vodka, syrup, and lemon juice. Top with club soda. Stir, garnish, and enjoy!

BLUEBERRY LEMONADE

If only all of life was quite so gloriously simple. Just like the Summer Kiss, this is fantastically refreshing and uses all the key ingredients of a cocktail— but elevated to the next world, especially in late summer, by using beautiful hand-picked blueberries. This is another cocktail we popped into a can.

1 ½ oz   vodka
¾ oz   blueberry syrup, or simple syrup
               with blueberries muddled in
1 ¼ oz   freshly squeezed lemon juice
1 ½ oz   club soda
               lemon slice, few fresh
                  blueberries, for garnish

Glass: good-size tumbler or tall Collins

Add vodka, syrup, and lemon juice to an ice-filled cocktail shaker. Shake until chilled and strain into a glass with ice. Top with club soda and stir gently. Garnish and enjoy!

GIN FIZZ

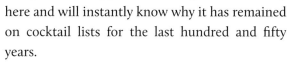

Another of the old-school cocktails that has stood the test of time. This is a close relation to the Tom Collins, with the simple addition of egg whites to provide the slightly more decadent frothy top and make the drink a little richer all the way through. There are lots of variations—some people put a whole egg in for a golden fizz, or champagne or sparkling wine to make it a diamond fizz! No matter how you make it, you're drinking a bit of history here and will instantly know why it has remained on cocktail lists for the last hundred and fifty years.

1 ½ oz	Cloudberry Gin
½ oz	lemon juice
½ oz	simple syrup
¾ oz	egg white
2–3	dashes of Cloudberry Bitters
	fresh spruce tip (in season),
	lemon slice, for garnish

Glass: *tall Collins*

Put all ingredients except bitters in a cocktail shaker and dry shake (without ice) for 15 to 20 seconds. Add ice and shake again until chilled. Strain over tall glass filled with ice. Top with Cloudberry Bitters, garnish, and enjoy.

CHAMBORD GIN FIZZ

Thanks to the raspberry liqueur, this makes a really pretty version of the classic Gin Fizz—a quick and easy twist.

2 oz	Seaweed Gin
½ oz	raspberry liqueur
½ oz	simple syrup
½ oz	freshly squeezed lemon juice
	club soda, to taste

Glass: *rocks*

Fill your glass with ice. Fill your cocktail shaker with ice. Pour the Seaweed Gin over it. Add remaining ingredients except the club soda. Shake well until chilled, but no more than 20 seconds. Strain into your glass and top with soda. Enjoy.

TOM COLLINS

Another historically proven classic cocktail. It's all about the gin. We get a little bit fancy by using fresh rosemary in our syrup. It does add another subtle layer of complexity. With the little sprinkle of Cloudberry Bitters on top, the drink is elevated to a perfectly held-together cocktail that will stand the test of time. And, yes, we have put this in a can too!

1 ½ oz	Seaweed Gin
½ oz	simple syrup
½ oz	lemon juice
2 oz	club soda
	rosemary sprig, lemon wedge, for garnish

Glass: *Collins (most definitely!)*

Put ice, gin, syrup, and lemon juice in cocktail shaker. Shake for 10 to 12 seconds. Strain contents into ice-filled glass. Top with club soda and stir gently. Garnish and enjoy!

RHUBARB REFRESHER

Mint works beautifully with our Rhubarb Vodka, as it blends the bite of the rhubarb and hint of partridgeberry to form the desired base for a classic sour. It's another delicious, long, refreshing cocktail for sipping outdoors on glorious summer nights.

1 ½ oz   Rhubarb Vodka

½ oz   simple syrup

½ oz   freshly squeezed lime juice

3   mint leaves

2–3 oz   club soda

Glass: *Collins or tumbler, or any large glass*

Fill your shaker with ice and pour vodka over. Add syrup and lime juice. Shake well for up to 10 seconds, and strain into a glass over ice. Add mint and muddle. Top with club soda. Gently stir, and enjoy.

CUBA LIBRE

I love a Cuba Libre and I chuckle when I say or think it, because really it is just a rum and coke—see highball section—with a wallop of fresh lime to give it zip. This means I can be a hardcore "bayman" and ask for rum and coke, but then I tend to wreck the charade by asking for half a lime to squeeze into it. Fortunately, everyone is kindly indulgent. You can't beat a rum and coke, but you do need to decide how much rum and how much coke you really want.

1 ½ oz	Gunpowder & Rose Rum
½ oz	freshly squeezed lime juice
2 oz	cola (Coke or Pepsi)
	lime slice, for garnish

Glass: *rocks*

Fill glass with ice. Add rum and lime juice, and top with cola. Stir gently. Garnish and enjoy!

GIN BASIL SMASH

———

Unsurprisingly, this is a relatively new addition to the cocktail canon, having been invented in Berlin in 2008. By adding basil to a cocktail, you are immediately elevated to the super hip, especially when you're using wonderfully handcrafted spirits.

Be more generous than you think you should, so you can get the "basil blast." The Seaweed Gin somehow works better than the Cloudberry Gin, perhaps due to its salinity and savoury notes that sit so well with the basil.

4–5	basil leaves
2 oz	Seaweed Gin
¾ oz	freshly squeezed lemon juice
½ oz	simple syrup
	splash club soda
	fresh basil leaf, lemon slice, for garnish

Glass: *rocks, or go wild with a coupe*

Muddle basil in cocktail shaker. Add all other ingredients and shake with ice until chilled. Strain into tumbler filled with crushed ice. Top with club soda. Garnish and enjoy!

DIRTY MOJITO

The word mojito takes my mind immediately to hot places with palm trees. Such a great drink with its fresh mint mixed with fresh lime, a bit of sugar and, most importantly, the rum! It's incredibly light and refreshing and simply glorious.

To be authentic, we should use white rum, but our Gunpowder & Rose Rum is our chosen substitution with its amber colour providing the "dirt." I think of the Gin Basil Smash and this mojito as herb siblings—both beautiful, clean, and pure.

4–5	mint leaves
½ oz	simple syrup
1 ½ oz	Gunpowder & Rose Rum
¾ oz	freshly squeezed lime juice
1 ½ oz	club soda
2–3	dashes of Sweet Gale & Wild Rose Bitters
	lime wedge, fresh mint leaf, for garnish

Glass: *Collins or a tumbler*

Put mint and syrup in cocktail shaker and muddle mint gently. Add remaining ingredients to shaker with ice and shake. Strain into tall glass over ice. Top with club soda and stir gently. Add bitters and garnish.

CRACKLIN' ROSE

This is similar to the Summer Kiss, but we've swapped the strawberries for raspberries and discovered it seems to go better with the straight vodka. I think it allows the taste of the raspberries to come through more. It's super simple to make and you'll be sipping away in no time. The red raspberries with the green mint creates a beautiful contrast.

1 ½ oz   vodka
½ oz   freshly squeezed lemon juice
½ oz   raspberry syrup (or ½ oz simple
          syrup with 4 muddled
          raspberries)
1 ½ oz   club soda
          whole raspberry, fresh mint leaf,
          for garnish

Glass: *rocks or tumbler*

Put all ingredients in a tumbler filled with ice. Stir well and garnish. If you fancy, you can shake this. Either way, enjoy!

LEMON DROP

———

When I was younger, this was my constant go-to for a cocktail. I could whip them up anywhere and everywhere and share them with however many people were around. My proportions varied, but everyone seemed to love its freshness and purity; it always makes you feel more enervated and ready to enjoy the party.

It's easy to turn it into a quick and easy shot, with 1 oz vodka, ½ oz simple syrup, and ½ oz freshly squeezed lemon. Stir or shake over ice and share.

	Lemon wedge (optional)
¼ tsp	sugar
2 oz	vodka
1 oz	freshly squeezed lemon juice
1 oz	simple syrup
	lemon slice

Glass: *If you want to be fancy, go for a martini glass.*

Run lemon wedge around rim of glass, then roll lemon-edged rim in sugar. Add all ingredients to an ice-filled cocktail shaker and shake until chilled. Strain into your martini glass and garnish. Enjoy!

CHERRY JANE'S LAST DANCE

Not quite Mary Jane's Last Dance, this is a cherry-based twist on vodka, lime, and soda. It has great colour thanks to the cherry and is sweetened by the cherry liqueur rather than syrup. If you're a cherry fan at all, you've got to give this one a spin! The lime does counteract the cherry intensity, leaving a light, slightly complex cocktail. Delightful.

1 ½ oz	vodka
1 ½ oz	cherry liqueur
½ oz	cherry juice
¼ oz	freshly squeezed lime juice
¾ oz	club soda
	maraschino cherry, for garnish

Glass: *Collins*

Add all ingredients to a shaker filled with ice and shake for 10 seconds. Strain into glass, over ice. Garnish and enjoy.

A CERTAIN DELIGHT

This is an eclectic selection that is bit more gin-based and full of drinks that you might not consider—little twists on a classic, or those that have come back into fashion. They should bring you a little smile of delight; if not, you'll have to pass them to the person sitting next to you.

Cocktails are extraordinary in that there are different variations of similar themes, or radical departures. This where all the fun is—experimenting, finding what you love and then what your friends and family love. And when you find cocktails that bring a smile to everyone's face, ones that help the chat get a little more involved, a little louder, you can sit back, take in the moment, and savour it. These are the perfect moments, and we all deserve as many as we can find.

CLOVER CLUB

———

This historic cocktail lost its gloss and place on bar menus only to be revived when the Clover Club Bar opened in Brooklyn in 2008, one of the finest cocktail bars in New York and the rest of the Eastern United States. The drink has never looked back.

It is a classic sour with a raspberry twist, so isn't quite as citrusy as a lot of its close relations, but you'll still be drinking a bit of history. We top it off with some Cloudberry Bitters for a little extra zing.

2–3	fresh raspberries
¼ oz	raspberry liqueur
1 ½ oz	Cloudberry Gin
¼ oz	sweet vermouth
¼ oz	dry vermouth
½ oz	freshly squeezed lemon juice
¾ oz	egg white
2–3	dashes of Cloudberry Bitters
	raspberry, for garnish

Glass: *coupe*

1. Put ice in your glass to chill. Muddle raspberries and liqueur in the cocktail shaker.
2. Add gin, vermouths, juice, and egg white. Dry shake (without ice) for 20 to 30 seconds.
3. Add ice to your cocktail shaker. Shake again until chilled, but be careful not to shake long enough for the ice to start to melt.
4. Empty ice from coupe glass and strain the mix into it. Top with bitters. Use a toothpick to pull through the drops of bitters to make pretty patterns on the surface. Garnish and enjoy.

PERISCOPE

There is a working periscope from World War II in the Crow's Nest Officers' Club in St. John's, founded in 1942 while the navy was protecting the supply lines between North America and the United Kingdom. If you are lucky enough to visit the Crow's Nest and use the periscope, you get a magnificent view of the harbour from the periscope, which runs up through the club's ceiling.

While the Periscope cocktail won't give you greater vision physically, it might well do the trick metaphysically, using a classic gin sour recipe with elderflower liqueur. The elderflower adds depth, nestling on the bakeapple of the gin to create a multi-flavoured and layered cocktail, held together with a bit of foam and body from the egg white. It's another impressive cocktail you can easily wow everyone with!

1 ½ oz	Cloudberry Gin
1 oz	elderflower liqueur
½ oz	simple syrup
½ oz	freshly squeezed lemon juice
½ oz	egg white
2–3	dashes of Cloudberry Bitters
	lemon peel, for garnish

Glass: *martini*

Put ice in martini glass to chill. Dry shake everything but the bitters, without ice, in a cocktail shaker for 15 seconds. Add ice to the shaker and shake for another 15 seconds. Empty ice from the now-chilled martini glass and strain mix into it. Top with bitters, garnish, and enjoy.

THE GOLDRUSH

A straight-to-the-point classic sour, and unlike the Aquavit Sour, which uses egg white to bind it together, this uses honey syrup, which is just a bit richer than a standard syrup and negates the need of egg. We've also opted to pour this over a large ice cube, to keep the temperature cool and make it a slightly more robust drink for the connoisseur. The mint helps freshen it up while, along with the cinnamon, adding a little mystery to the cocktail.

2–3	fresh mint leaves
pinch	ground cinnamon
¾ oz	honey syrup
2 oz	Aquavit
½ oz	freshly squeezed lemon juice
	cinnamon stick, fresh mint leaf, for garnish

Glass: *tumbler or rocks*

Muddle together the mint leaves, cinnamon, and honey syrup in a cocktail shaker. Add ice, Aquavit, and lemon juice. Shake until chilled and strain into tumbler with a large ice cube. Garnish and enjoy!

AQUAVIT SOUR

This is our twist on the classic Whisky Sour, which remains among the most venerable of all cocktails, having been a standard at any bar since the 1860s. The three classic ingredients—spirit, lemon, and simple syrup—are brought together with the egg white to make the drink a little more rich, smooth, and velvety, with froth on top. There is a reason it has lasted so long.

1 ½ oz	Aquavit
½ oz	simple syrup
½ oz	freshly squeezed lemon juice
1 oz	egg white
2–3	dashes of Chaga & Chanterelle Bitters

Glass: *a lovely coupe or a stemmed wineglass*

Chill your glass by putting in ice. Put everything but the bitters into a cocktail shaker and dry shake, without ice, for 20 to 30 seconds. Add ice and shake again—just until chilled. Empty the ice from your now-chilled glass and strain mix into it. Top with bitters, spread equally across the top of the foam. Pull a toothpick through the drops of bitters to make pretty patterns on the surface. Fun and games.

THYME ON OUR SIDE

———

While Mick Jagger still seems to have time on his side, we can all have a bit of Thyme on Our Side (couldn't resist). This is another twist on the classic sour, but using oleo-saccharum—Latin for oil sugar—which is citrus peels marinated in sugar. Added levels of citrus notes come through oils of the skin and not just the flesh of the fruit, so it is definitely worth the effort.

½ oz   oleo-saccharum (recipe below)
1 ½ oz   Cloudberry Gin
½ oz   sweet vermouth
½ oz   simple syrup
           fresh mint leaf, fresh sprig
              thyme, for garnish

Glass: *coupe*

To create oleo-saccharum, you've got to be slightly ahead of the game, as it takes 6 to 24 hours to marinate. Peel lemons, oranges, and limes with a peeler, avoiding the white pith as much as possible. A cup will do. Add ¾ cup of sugar. Mix vigorously. Leave to marinate. Strain the ingredients, squishing the peels as much as you can.

Place ice in mixing glass. Add all ingredients. Stir until chilled. Strain into coupe, garnish, and enjoy.

PAPER PLANE

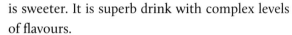

This really is named after M.I.A.'s fantastic song "Paper Planes," and is now a constant party staple, originally created to help launch a new Chicago cocktail bar in 2007. The cocktail was such a success it flew on to the list of every self-respecting cocktail bar.

It is usually made with bourbon, but once again we've swapped in our Aquavit, which I think works even better. Traditionally, most cocktail bars use Aperol, and while I generally prefer Campari, the Aperol works well as it is sweeter. It is superb drink with complex levels of flavours.

¾ oz	Aquavit
¾ oz	Aperol
¾ oz	Triple Sec
¾ oz	freshly squeezed lemon
2–3	dashes of Cloudberry Bitters
	lemon peel, for garnish

Glass: *coupe, martini, or any long-stemmed glass*

Put ice in your coupe glass to chill. Fill cocktail shaker with ice and add everything but the bitters. Shake until chilled. Empty ice from your glass and strain mix into it. Top with bitters. Garnish with lemon twist—twist your thin strip of lemon peel—and enjoy!

A BOY NAMED SUE

As the song goes, life can be tough if you are a boy named Sue. Each summer we, like everyone here, have that enviable dilemma of a surfeit of blueberries, so we have to try use them in every drink. This is usually easy, but it was tough going to incorporate the blueberry syrup in a classic gin sour. We tested, tried, and added all sorts of things. Finally, by adding a small amount of dry vermouth, we came up with a surprisingly rewarding drink that made the endeavour worthwhile!

1 ½ oz	Seaweed Gin
⅓ oz	dry vermouth
½ oz	blueberry syrup
½ oz	freshly squeezed lemon juice
2	dashes of Seaweed & Nettle Bitters
	sprig fresh thyme, for garnish

Glass: *Tumbler*

Fill cocktail shaker with ice. Add gin, vermouth, blueberry syrup, and lemon juice to the shaker. Shake until chilled. Strain mix into a tumbler with ice. Top with bitters and garnish. Enjoy.

BEES KNEES

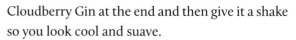

Though Bees Knees was created in Paris, it quickly became a hit in the United States, where it was regarded as superb. This is very close to the classic gin sour that uses a straight simple syrup. Our honey syrup gives a richer and deeper taste that doesn't become overwhelming because of the lemon. It is great for parties, as you can premix the lemon and honey syrup, add the Cloudberry Gin at the end and then give it a shake so you look cool and suave.

2 oz   Cloudberry Gin
½ oz   honey syrup
¾ oz   freshly squeezed lemon juice
          lemon peel, for garnish

Glass: coupe, martini, or any stemmed glass

Put ice in your glass to chill. Fill cocktail shaker with ice. Add all ingredients and shake until chilled. Empty the ice from the coupe glass and strain mix into it. Garnish with a lemon twist—twist your thin strip of lemon peel—and enjoy.

RED SKY AT NIGHT

"Red sky at night, sailor's delight" means the next day should have good weather, whereas "red sky in morning" is a "sailor's warning." I grew up in the middle of the country, very landlocked, and we always said "shepherd's delight."

Thanks to the cherry liqueur and other ingredients in here, we get the perfect "red sky at night" drink that gets a little kick from spicy ginger beer. The sweetness of the cherry liqueur balances the spice. A refreshing long drink that works for every colour of the sky.

1 ½ oz	Rhubarb Vodka
½ oz	cherry liqueur
½ oz	cherry liquid (juice from a maraschino cherry jar)
½ oz	freshly squeezed lime juice
½ oz	ginger beer
1 ½ oz	club soda
	maraschino cherry, lime slice, for garnish

Glass: *tall Collins*

Fill a tall glass with ice. Add all the ingredients in the written order (alcohol is always first). Stir gently. Garnish and enjoy.

THE IN-CLOUD

Who needs to be with the *in* crowd when it's much more fun to sit apart, have a good conversation, and relax? The In-Cloud, however, is something you do want—a long refreshing take on a sour, adding the slightly sweeter bitterness of Aperol, richer honey syrup, and a dash of elderflower liqueur. Once you have it in your hand, everything slows down and you can investigate all the flavours and catch up with an old friend.

1 oz	Cloudberry Gin
½ oz	Aperol
¼ oz	elderflower liqueur
½ oz	honey syrup
¾ oz	freshly squeezed lemon juice
3 oz	club soda
1–2	dashes of Cloudberry Bitters
	maraschino cherry, lemon slice, for garnish

Glass: *tall Collins*

Fill cocktail shaker with ice. Add gin, Aperol, liqueur, syrup, and lemon juice to the shaker. Shake until chilled. Strain mix into a tall glass filled with ice. Top with club soda and stir. Add bitters, garnish, and enjoy.

BELL ISLAND ICED TEA

———

Who needs Long Island when you can gaze at Bell Island across the bay? This is our take on the classic Long Island Iced Tea, which, I do admit, was once one of my favourite drinks. With the wonderful naïveté of youth, I was convinced it was the most potent drink on the cocktail list, as it had at least four different spirits in it, and it wasn't expensive—a win-win for a young, enthusiastic cocktail drinker. It took me an embarrassing amount of time to realize the bar staff actually measured smaller amounts of each spirit, and it was only as strong as other strong cocktails, about two ounces.

I still have a soft spot for it, so we came up with Bell Island Iced Tea using three of our spirits and Triple Sec. And, yes, it takes me wistfully back to those youthful days.

½ oz	vodka
½ oz	Cloudberry Gin
½ oz	Gunpowder & Rose Rum
½ oz	Triple Sec
¾ oz	cola
¾ oz	freshly squeezed lemon juice

Glass: *tall Collins*

Fill tall glass with ice. Pour all ingredients into the glass. Stir gently to mix. Enjoy!

BOLDER

As you wisely assume, the drinks here are all a little bigger and deeper in their flavour, and not necessarily for the faint of heart. That said, there's also a lot of subtlety and complexity in these drinks, which are all deeply rewarding for those who don't want shy and retiring cocktails; they are lots of fun and always great for a party.

CABLE CAR

The Cable Car has already become a contemporary classic, which is technically an oxymoron. To clarify, it is a new addition to the cocktail world, first made in San Francisco in the late 1990s to celebrate their cable cars. It has since appeared on almost every hip cocktail bar menu. Its allure is still growing, partly because there is a wide range of craft-distilled spiced rums out there, including our Gunpowder & Rose Rum, which, while technically spiced, is not spiced in the more conventional way.

The combined sweetness of an orange liqueur, such as Triple Sec, mixed with the syrup, is counteracted by the acidity of fresh lemon. This allows for the complexity of rum to be showcased as it interacts with the orange flavours.

1 ½ oz	Gunpowder & Rose Rum
½ oz	Triple Sec
½ oz	simple syrup
½ oz	freshly squeezed lemon juice
	orange peel, for garnish

Glass: good solid rocks glass that holds a big ice cube

Add all ingredients to a cocktail shaker with ice. Shake and strain into tumbler with large ice cube. Singe orange peel for extra flavour and use it for garnish.

SALTY SAILOR

This is an intensely citrus drink, with a rare mix of fresh lemon and lime juice, so it is only for citrus lovers who will be all puckered up with joy. The pinch of salt, along with the bitters, helps the citrus and gin flavours meld together. Try one with salt and one without to taste the difference.

2 oz	Seaweed Gin
pinch	salt
½ oz	simple syrup
¾ oz	freshly squeezed lime juice
¼ oz	freshly squeezed lemon juice
1–2	dashes of Seaweed & Nettle Bitters
	lime slice, for garnish

Glass: *long-stemmed, ideally a coupe*

Put ice in a shaker. Add gin, salt, syrup, and juices. Shake well for no more than 10 seconds. Strain into a chilled glass. Drop in the bitters, garnish, and enjoy!

HARVEST MOON

This immediately makes me think of Neil Young and his classic album *Harvest Moon*. A fantastic sipping cocktail with surprising complexity of flavours, thanks in part to the mint, honey syrup, and—the real clincher—the bakeapple jam. And there's something wonderful about a mint leaf floating on top of a cocktail—I always eat it. As the name suggests, this is a fall drink, but it stands up to every season with a surprising mix of lightness and warmth.

5	mint leaves
¾ oz	honey simple syrup
2 oz	Gunpowder & Rose Rum
½ oz	freshly squeezed lime juice
½ tsp	bakeapple jam
1–2	dashes of Sweet Gale & Wild Rose Bitters
	fresh mint leaf, bakeapple berry, or a bit of jam for garnish

Glass: *your fancy coupe, or anything with a stem*

Put mint and syrup in cocktail shaker. Muddle mint gently. Fill shaker with ice. Add rum, juice, and jam. Shake for 15 to 20 seconds. Strain into your chilled glass. Drop in bitters and garnish.

ESPRESSO MARTINI

This seems to be the drink of the decade so far, with its many variations. It is wonderful after a long day and will give you the caffeine shot and fine bit of spirit to lift you up. Typically, espresso martinis are made with vodka, but we wanted ours to be a bit richer, so went for the Chaga Rum. Always a fantastic treat.

2 oz	Chaga Rum
½ oz	coffee liqueur
½ oz	simple syrup
1 oz	espresso
	shaved chocolate or few coffee beans, for garnish

Glass: *martini or coupe*

Add all ingredients to an ice-filled cocktail shaker. Shake well, until chilled. Strain into a chilled martini glass. Garnish and enjoy.

HONEYSUCKLE

Honey syrup seems to blend perfectly with Chaga Rum, which has caramel-ized honey in it. (Ironically, caramelizing the honey makes it more bitter, helping to decrease the sweetness of the rum.) The lime juice then lifts it all up again. This is a deeply satisfying drink.

2 oz	Chaga Rum
¾ oz	honey syrup
¾ oz	freshly squeezed lime juice
1–2	dashes of Chaga & Chanterelle Bitters
	lime slice, for garnish

Glass: *large tumbler or rocks*

Put all ingredients in a cocktail shaker. Shake with ice until chilled. Put large ice cube in tumbler and strain drink into it. Garnish and enjoy.

MAN O' WAR

———

The original uses bourbon, but as the name celebrates an extraordinary racehorse that won 20 out of 21 races, we've just hijacked the name and swapped our Aquavit for the bourbon. This is a serious cocktail with Triple Sec and sweet vermouth, which are there to counterbalance the lemon juice. With a few drops of Sweet Gale & Rose Bitters, you're on to an absolute winner.

2 oz	Aquavit
½ oz	Triple Sec
½ oz	sweet vermouth
⅓ oz	freshly squeezed lemon juice
2–3	dashes of Sweet Gale & Wild Rose Bitters
	lemon strip, for garnish

Glass: *martini is perfect, or coupe*

Add all ingredients to an ice-filled cocktail shaker. Shake until chilled. Strain into a chilled martini glass. Twist and singe strip, garnish, and enjoy.

HALLO SPACEBOY

This is one of those slightly unusual cocktails where you think it shouldn't work, but you keep tweaking until it suddenly locks into place. The idea of mixing green Chartreuse and Cherry Liqueur screams "no" to me—much like the idea of welcoming a "spaceboy" into the house.

This is one of those cocktails to boldly go where few have been before.

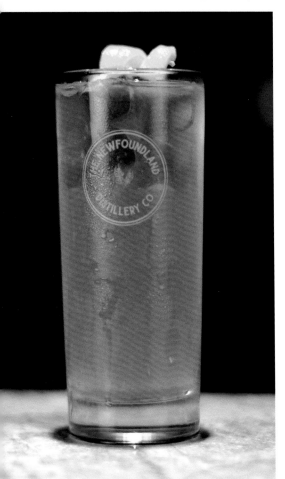

1 oz	Aquavit
¼ oz	green Chartreuse
¼ oz	cherry liqueur
¼ oz	simple syrup
½ oz	freshly squeezed lime juice
1 ½ oz	club soda
	lemon strip, for garnish

Glass: tall Collins would be perfect

Add everything but club soda to an ice-filled cocktail shaker. Shake until chilled. Strain into ice-filled Collins glass. Add soda. Twist and singe lemon strip, garnish, and enjoy.

BOOZIER

This section is exactly as it sounds and features classic cocktails that, simply put, are booze-forward—the bulk of the cocktail should be handcrafted liquor.

These drinks really focus on showcasing the quality of the spirits. Remember that they can surprise inexperienced or overly enthusiastic cocktail drinkers. As a rule, the first boozy cocktail is fantastic, usually so good you immediately would like a second. A second might be fine, but a third might bring a quicker end to the evening.

This section is home to the martini, Manhattan, and Old Fashioned, which are among the most loved and best-known cocktails, with endless small and subtle variations. There are even cocktail books dedicated solely to each of them, but we're keeping it simple with just a few variations.

CLASSIC MARTINI

———

Shaken or stirred? It should always be gently stirred (caressed, even) and definitely not shaken, as you bruise the booze that way. The only reason James Bond liked his shaken, I'm assuming, is that he didn't have the lovingly hand-crafted boutique gins and vodkas currently available.

Now to the real martini dilemma—how dry do you like it? Lemon peel or olive? There is no right or wrong, although those who "know" about drinks like a dryer martini. My favourite, at the moment, is a Seaweed Gin Martini, with the finest olive you can find. The best way to perfect your martini is to vary the amount of vermouth until you have found what you like. Be sure to

chill the glass and ensure the gin is super cold, by gently stirring it in a cocktail shaker. If you are a great forward-thinker, you could even keep a bottle in the freezer.

2 ½ oz Seaweed Gin
¼ oz   dry vermouth (Dolin or another hip vermouth, or old stalwart Martini Dry) lemon peel, olive (big, green Castelvetrano recommended), for garnish

Glass: In a perfect world you will have a lovely, styling martini glass. If not, go for the widest, most shallow glass you have, ideally with a stem.

Put ice cubes in your martini glass to chill. Put ice in your cocktail shaker. Pour in gin and vermouth, but if you like a really dry martini, don't put the vermouth in yet. If you like a wet martini, double the vermouth. Stir gently, trying to cover the ice with the gin, for 20 seconds or so. The shaker should feel cold. Discard the ice in the martini glass.

For a really dry martini, pour a little vermouth into the glass, swirl it around, and discard. Use a strainer to hold back the ice and pour chilled cocktail into the glass. (If you don't have a strainer, a saucer will do the trick.)

Place olive, preferably on a cocktail stick, into the glass gently, and the lemon peel. Enjoy.

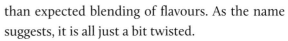

BITTER, SWEET, AND TWISTED

———

A variation on the martini, this cocktail uses our Rhubarb Vodka with a surprisingly generous amount of dry vermouth to create a slightly sweeter  than expected blending of flavours. As the name suggests, it is all just a bit twisted.

The most fun way to find your favourites of the many martini variations is to keep exploring the different spirits and tweaking the proportions until they are perfect for you.

2 oz	Rhubarb Vodka
¼ oz	dry vermouth
	tiny gherkin, pearl onion,
	maraschino cherry, for garnish

Glass: *martini*

Add ingredients to a cocktail shaker with ice. Stir for 20 to 30 seconds. Strain into chilled martini glass. Garnish as indicated. Told you it was twisted!

BRONX

———

In the 1930s, this was one of the top three most popular cocktails, along with the martini and Manhattan. While still a proper boozy drink, this really is a "perfect" martini, using both sweet and dry vermouths and freshly squeezed orange juice, which makes it a longer drink. The juice lightens the intensity of all the spirits and so is perhaps a great gateway into martinis.

2 oz	Cloudberry Gin
¼ oz	dry vermouth
¼ oz	sweet vermouth
1 oz	freshly squeezed orange juice
2	dashes of Classic Bitters
¼ tsp	orange zest, for garnish

Glass: *martini or coupe*

Put ice in a shaker. Add all ingredients and shake until chilled. Strain into chilled martini glass. Add bitters and orange zest on top. Enjoy.

MANHATTAN

Some people think this might be the first modern cocktail—Philip Greene even wrote a book arguing this. It is, indisputably, a classic and has been

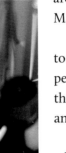

around since the 1870s, when it became the trendy Manhattan socialite drink.

The key is the addition of a bit of sweet vermouth to bourbon or an American whiskey, which tempers the more robust nature of the whiskey, giving the cocktail more sophistication and complexity and ultimately making it supremely palatable.

We make the Manhattan with our Aquavit, which is the closest spirit we have to any kind of whisky. Other than that, we've stuck to the traditional recipe and think this Manhattan, via Clarke's Beach, is right up there with the very best. Test, tweak, and keep trying until you get the version you love! You can even try different bitters to bring out more flavours.

2 oz	Aquavit
½ oz	sweet vermouth
2–3	dashes of Chaga & Chanterelle Bitters
	orange peel, maraschino cherry, for garnish

Glass: *good solid rocks*

Place ingredients in a tumbler with a large ice cube and stir. Top with bitters. Singe orange peel and use as garnish along with a cherry. Cheers!

RUMHATTAN

———

This is a cunning twist on the Manhattan using the deep, rich flavours of our Chaga Rum—excellent for the colder months.

Key to a Manhattan is the quality of the spirit and the sweet vermouth—we always go for the best we can get our hands on. Remember that many cocktails are made to enhance the enjoyment of the spirit, so by combining a few crucial ingredients you can bring out its delicate flavours.

Bitters are an essential flourish, much like having salt with your chips. Also, you can now easily buy superb maraschino cherries that have been marinated in all sorts of spirits—it's great fun finding your favourite.

2 oz	Chaga Rum
⅓ oz	sweet vermouth
2	dashes of Chaga & Chanterelle Bitters
	orange peel, for garnish

Glass: *martini, or something close*

Put ice in your shaker. Pour in rum and vermouth. Stir with a cocktail spoon for 20 seconds to mix. Strain into a chilled martini glass and add the bitters. Add garnish and enjoy.

HIGH HORSE

The name says it all—when you're on your high horse, inevitably you hit the ground with a bump. This is a Rumhattan with cherry bells and whistles and is perfect for when you come in from the cold, or just need something deeply comforting to nurture you back to warmth and happiness. This was created by the super hip and trendy Death & Co cocktail bar in New York as a nod to George Washington, who loved rum and cherries.

1 ½ oz	Chaga Rum
½ oz	brandy
½ oz	cherry liqueur
½ oz	sweet vermouth
1	dash of Classic Bitters
	maraschino cherry, for garnish

Glass: *martini or coupe*

Put ice in a mixing glass. Pour in all liquid ingredients and stir until liquid is chilled. Strain into martini glass. Add bitters and garnish to your taste.

OTTERBURY FASHIONED

Otterbury (as in Otterbury Road in Clarke's Beach) is our take on the venerable, classic Old Fashioned, a favourite of Don Draper from the drama series *Mad Men*, which famously promoted cocktail drinking at pretty much all hours of the day. Don knew his way around a drinks cabinet.

Apparently, this is one of the oldest cocktails—from the early 1800s—and was, I suspect, a way to make bourbon slightly more palatable. Now people take it very seriously indeed and use the best bourbons, or other spirits, to make the ultimate Old Fashioned. We've selected our Aquavit.

You can make this the old-fashioned way, building the drink in a tumbler, using a sugar cube laced with bitters, then stirring it with spirit and water, followed by the rest of your spirit and ice. But this new, slightly easier way is my preference.

2 oz	Aquavit
½ oz	molasses syrup
2 ½	dashes of Chaga & Chanterelle Bitters
	orange zest, strip of orange, slightly burnt, for garnish

Glass: *rocks or tumbler would be perfect.*

Place one large ice cube in your glass. Pour the Aquavit, syrup, and bitters into mixing glass. Stir for at least 15 seconds, and strain into your glass. Top with zest and garnish with orange peel. Enjoy!

MAPLE RUM OLD FASHIONED

A great take on the Old Fashioned. This time we have a match made in heaven—the classic Canadian version that's made with maple syrup, with the Newfoundland and Labrador adaptation that has rum. We use our Chaga Rum, which has a great depth of flavour, its earthiness matching the maple simple syrup. The bitters bring the drink alive.

2 oz	Chaga Rum
¼ oz	dry vermouth
⅓ oz	maple syrup
2–3	dashes of Chaga & Chanterelle Bitters
	orange peel, maraschino cherry, for garnish

Glass: a good solid rocks glass

Pour all ingredients into an ice-filled mixing glass. Stir to chill. Strain into a tumbler with a large ice cube. Stir gently. Singe your orange peel and use as garnish with the cherry.

CLASSIC DAIQUIRI

Daiquiris started in Cuba (there is actually a place called Daiquiri) and then became Ernest Hemingway's drink when he lived in Key West, Florida. They are perfect for hot sunny days or for dreaming about hot sunny days. Rum is the drink of the Caribbean (and this province) and is the key ingredient. Our Gunpowder & Rose Rum works well, and the fresh acidity of the lime mixed with and balanced by sugar creates perfect harmony for this most glorious drink.

Sadly, Daiquiris have a very bad name because of all sorts of bizarre variations and colours and odd ready-made concoctions that you shouldn't be touching, let alone drinking.

1 ½ oz	Gunpowder & Rose Rum
½ oz	simple syrup
½ oz	freshly squeezed lime juice
2–3	dashes of Seaweed & Nettle Bitters
	lime slice, for garnish

Glass: *coupe or long-stemmed glass*

Add ingredients to an ice-filled cocktail shaker and shake. Strain into a chilled coupe glass. Top with bitters, garnish, and enjoy!

ATLANTIC 75

We came up with the Atlantic 75 during a partnership with the Nova Scotia winery Benjamin Bridge, as a local twist on the French 75. Benjamin Bridge and other wineries in Nova Scotia are now making supremely good sparkling wines, and their vintage selection can compete with proper Champagnes. Climate change has warmed the weather and lengthened the growing season, so the climate and soil, particularly in the Gaspereau Valley, are similar to the Champagne area in Northern France.

The cocktail was named by a New York barman after the famous, powerful French 75 mm cannons used during World War 1. The cocktails were an instant success, and customers who enjoyed them rapidly and repeatedly found themselves in a terrible state the next day.

The Atlantic 75 is one of my favourites; you've got the extra hit of gin with a bit of lemon to set off the lovely effervescence of the sparkling wine—it's very clean and refreshing. It's a drink to be shared, as you don't want to leave a bottle of sparkling wine hanging around. And you also want to temper your enthusiasm and remember how they came up with the name.

½ oz	simple syrup
½ oz	freshly squeezed lemon juice
1 ½ oz	Cloudberry Gin
2 oz	Nova Scotia dry sparkling wine

Glass: *ideally a flute, or the tallest, narrowest wineglass you can find*

Put ice in the bottom of cocktail shaker, jam jar, or other shaker. Add syrup, juice, and gin. Shake well, until the shaker is cool, about 15 seconds. Pour into glass, using a strainer (or fork or other implement to keep ice out of glass). Top up with sparkling wine.

You can mix multiple batches of the base (syrup, lemon, and gin) at once, so if you're serving four people, increase it four times.

SEAWEED MARGARITA

This is our riff on the classic Margarita, and we've switched the tequila for our Seaweed Gin. It doesn't taste like tequila at all, but the slight salinity in the gin sits perfectly within the cocktail and allows the orange liqueur to come through.

We use a pinch of fantastic Newfoundland sea salt from Bonavista to give it that initial bite. You certainly can put the salted rim on your glass, but I find that overwhelming. If you're torn, you can always rim half the glass.

Margaritas should be cold and relatively short and intense, which makes them so invigorating.

	lime wedge
pinch	sea salt
1 ½ oz	Seaweed Gin
½ oz	orange liqueur
¾ oz	lime juice
½ oz	simple syrup
2–3	dashes of Seaweed & Nettle Bitters
	lime peel, for garnish

Glass: *coupe or tumbler—your call*

If desired, run lime wedge around half the rim of glass. Roll the lime-edged rim in salt. Pour liquid ingredients into an ice-filled cocktail shaker. Shake until chilled. Strain into your glass. Top with bitters. Garnish and enjoy!

FOR THE PALATE THAT'S CHOOSIER

This is the section where a few of my favourite cocktails are hiding. It's not that my palate is choosier, it's just that these are the divisive cocktails—ones you either love or don't want to be served *ever*.

Cocktails like the Negroni. I get totally excited by a Negroni, yet some of my family are baffled as to why anyone would enjoy one. Equally, eggnog makes me yawn, although most people I know think a proper eggnog is an amazing thing. A properly made one is infinitely superior to the carton version, I will admit, and I confess, I almost enjoy it. These sorts of dilemmas and different preferences generate some of the great joys of cocktails—there is always something for everyone. Be brave; you might find one of your new favourites here.

CAESAR

———

A Caesar makes me think of Sunday mornings after a fun Saturday night. Everyone is reminiscing and feeling a little bit jaded. A wonderful brunch is about to arrive and some bright spark has made a batch of Caesars, with their restorative goodness.

The Caesar is a close relation to the Bloody Mary, which is made using tomato juice, but the Caesar is a Canadian invention and much more popular here. Our twist here is to add Seaweed Gin, which works superbly, its salinity perfectly blending with a Clamato-based juice (look for good quality without

additives). The dry sherry creates full body and depth of taste that is profoundly satisfying.

Finally, for garnishes, you can really go all out with oysters or shrimp. We've been more practical, using homemade spicy pickled beans, which act as stirrers and are also great to snack on. A celery stick is another great alternative.

1 ½ oz	Seaweed Gin
½ oz	dry sherry
4 oz	Caesar mix (Walter Craft Caesar Mix preferred)
dash	celery salt
dash	Worcestershire sauce
dash	Tabasco
dash	Caesar spice (Walter Craft Caesar Rim preferred)
	spicy bean, lemon wedge, for garnish

Glass: *Collins or other tall glass*

If you would like to have the Caesar spice rim on your glass, pull lemon wedge around the rim of a tall glass, then dip the glass in your Caesar spice to rim the glass. If you're unsure, you can always just use the Caesar spice on half the rim. Fill glass with ice and add all ingredients. Stir well. Garnish and enjoy!

'TIL THE BITTER END

It can take a while to acquire the taste for Campari and Negronis. This is the best way to get there. The fresh juices and simple syrup bring down the stronger, bitter tastes of the Campari for a lovely, long, refreshing cocktail.

And, yes, this is one you want to keep enjoying. Like all great drinks, food, movies, and sporting games, it's not over until the glorious or bitter end.

1 oz	Cloudberry Gin
1 oz	Campari
½ oz	simple syrup
½ oz	freshly squeezed lemon juice
2 oz	freshly squeezed orange juice
	orange slice, for garnish

Glass: *rocks or good-sized tumbler*

Add all ingredients to a cocktail shaker with ice. Shake. Place large ice cube in your glass and strain drink into it. Garnish and enjoy!

NEW YORK SOUR

———

This one is a real looker, with the striking contrast of the red wine and the traditions of a typical sour—spirit, lemon juice, sugar, and egg white. It is surprisingly easy to pull off what is essentially the summer version of mulled wine. The trick here is to make the sour first, emulsifying the egg white in the shaker with all the ingredients except the wine.

1 ½ oz	Gunpowder & Rose Rum
½ oz	simple syrup
½ oz	freshly squeezed lemon juice
1 oz	egg white
2 oz	red wine
2	dashes of Sweet Gale & Wild Rose Bitters

Glass: *stemless wineglass or tumbler*

Pour rum, simple syrup, egg white, and juice into the shaker. Shake well for no more than 10 seconds. Add the ice and shake for another 10 seconds. Strain into a chilled glass. Using the back of a spoon, gently pour in wine and it will, amazingly, settle just below the froth of the egg white and above the rest of the mix. To make pretty patterns with the bitters, drop your dashes equidistant from each other and draw a cocktail stick through the bitters. Sit back and admire.

NEGRONI

This is one my favourites and an absolute classic with bitterness, sweetness, and botanicals sitting together so perfectly. Instant sophistication and also incredibly easy to make.

This drink was purportedly invented by Count Camillo Negroni in Florence when he asked the barman to make his usual Americano stronger, by replacing the club soda with gin. We like his thinking, as does the rest of the world. With this drink, you are an instant cocktail connoisseur.

1 oz	Cloudberry Gin
1 oz	Campari
1 oz	sweet vermouth
2–3	dashes of Sweet Gale & Wild Rose Bitters
	orange peel, thin strip

Glass: big, solid rocks glass or tumbler

Add all ingredients to a cocktail shaker with ice and stir. Place large ice cube in a tumbler (to slow the melting process and prevent it from diluting the wonderful flavours) and strain drink into it. Top with bitters. Singe orange peel by wafting it over a match or lighter for a few seconds, then gently squeeze the edges over the drink to release the oils. Pop it into the drink, sit back, and enjoy. If you are short on ice, you can get away with pouring all the ingredients over the ice in your glass, then stirring.

BOULEVARDIER

Another classic, and a simple twist on a Negroni to create a lovely winter version. We did wonder about changing the name as the Boulevardier is technically for the bourbon version and we use Aquavit. But I do love the idea of the decadent boulevardier strolling through the streets of Paris or Montreal and stopping at every café.

The Aquavit sits surprisingly well with the bitter flavours.

1 oz	Aquavit
1 oz	Campari
1 oz	sweet vermouth
2–3	dashes of Sweet Gale & Wild Rose Bitters
	orange peel, thin strip

Glass: *big, solid rocks glass or tumbler*

Add all ingredients to ice in a cocktail shaker and stir. Place large ice cube in a tumbler and strain drink into it. Top with bitters. Singe orange peel, then give a gentle squeeze of the edges over the drink to release the oils. Pop it into the drink, sit back, and enjoy.

NEWFOUNDLAND NEGRONI

Of course, we had to put our Gunpowder & Rose Rum into the Negroni instead of gin. I'm amazed how versatile the Negroni ingredients are—they seem to call out the key flavours of any base spirit yet still maintain the character and integrity of the original Negroni.

This rum version is another instant classic and perhaps helps with that crucial dilemma of which Negroni to have.

1 oz	Gunpowder & Rose Rum
1 oz	Campari
1 oz	sweet vermouth
2–3	dashes of Chaga & Chanterelle Bitters
	orange peel, thin strip

Glass: *solid rocks glass or tumbler*

Add all ingredients to a cocktail shaker with ice and stir. Place large ice cube in a tumbler and strain drink into it. Top with bitters. Singe orange peel, then give a gentle squeeze of the edges over the drink to release the oils. Pop it into the drink, sit back, and enjoy.

TARNISHED NAIL

This is our take on the Rusty Nail, which is bourbon and Drambuie. It was a bit of a classic cocktail from the sixties to the nineties and now seems to have fallen off cocktail lists. Apparently, the Rat Pack (Frank Sinatra et al.) loved it. There is something properly comforting about the Tarnished Nail. It is undoubtedly boozy and lets the spirits do all the talking.

Drambuie is a Scottish liqueur, based on whisky (the Scottish type) and honey, with the addition of herbs and spices. Its slightly sweeter notes sit very well with our Aquavit. We think it should return to the front row.

2 oz	Aquavit
1 oz	Drambuie
2–3	dashes of Chaga & Chanterelle Bitters
	lemon peel, thin strip

Glass: *big, solid rocks glass or tumbler*

Place all ingredients and ice in a cocktail shaker and stir. Place large ice cube in a tumbler and strain drink into it. Top with bitters. Singe lemon peel, then give a gentle squeeze of the edges over the drink to release the oils. Pop it into the drink, sit back, and enjoy.

EGGNOG (FOR TWO)

This is all about Christmas and sharing and whipping up the indulgence levels! It is deeply decadent and if you fancy it outside the Christmas season, you should definitely go for it.

Making eggnog properly is surprisingly easy, as all you have to do is put all the ingredients into a shaker or jar and shake vigorously.

This recipe is for two people: you really should be sharing this. It can be doubled as needed.

½ tsp	cinnamon
½ tsp	cloves
2	egg yolks
4 oz	Gunpowder & Rose Rum
5 oz	whole milk
2 oz	whipping cream
¾ oz	simple syrup
1	star of anise, pinch nutmeg, grated or ground, for garnish

Glass: *coupes, or any pair to make it easy to share*

Muddle cinnamon and cloves in top half of cocktail shaker. Place egg yolks, rum, milk, cream, and syrup in bottom half. Shake vigorously. Add ice and give it a quick, gentle shake to cool the liquid. Strain into glass and garnish. Lovely.

LONDON CALLING

This is another of my favourites (sorry, I do seem to have lots of favourites). I always think of the song, too, which makes me feel young and very rock 'n' roll, even before I've had a sip.

The sherry makes all the difference, giving the drink a little more body, depth, and complexity than the more straightforward sours.

1 ½ oz	Seaweed Gin
½ oz	dry sherry
½ oz	simple syrup
½ oz	freshly squeezed lemon juice
1–2	dashes of bitters

Glass: coupe

Add all ingredients to cocktail shaker with ice. Shake and strain into coupe. Add bitters and enjoy this very grown-up drink.

WHITE LADY

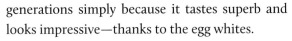

Another old-school cocktail, this one originated in London in the 1920s and has kept on going. It's a slightly fancier version of the Gin Fizz—adding Triple Sec allows you to reduce the simple syrup. This has been loved for generations simply because it tastes superb and looks impressive—thanks to the egg whites.

1 ½ oz	Seaweed Gin
¾ oz	Triple Sec
½ oz	simple syrup
¾ oz	freshly squeezed lemon juice
½	egg white
1	dash of bitters

Glass: martini or coupe

Pour all ingredients into a cocktail shaker without ice. Dry shake. Add ice and shake to cool. Strain into glass, add bitters, and enjoy this sophisticated drink.

FIDDLER'S GREEN

———

In a perfect world, this would be served with a couple of fine fiddlers playing "Saltwater Joys," a classic song in Newfoundland and Labrador that is learned by every budding violin player.

This is a riff on the classic White Lady but uses green Chartreuse instead of the Triple Sec, which does ramp up the botanical and flavour levels in the drink. You will either really love it or not love it at all. Definitely worth trying at least once, like almost all things in life.

1 ½ oz	Seaweed Gin
¼ oz	green Chartreuse
½ oz	simple syrup
¾ oz	freshly squeezed lime juice
½	egg white
1–2	dashes of Seaweed & Nettle Bitters

Glass: *coupe*

Pour all ingredients into a cocktail shaker without ice. Dry shake and then add ice. Shake to cool. Strain into coupe and add bitters.

CANADIANO

———

Our Cloudberry Gin makes the Americano cross the border and become a Canadiano! The drink originated as one of the early Campari cocktails in the 1860s in Milan, where Campari is produced. In the early 1930s, it became the Americano, perhaps to break into the American market. It is a classic Italian aperitif, with a good complexity of flavours, elongated by the club soda. The Italians are firm believers in the aperitif—it signifies the end of the working day, time to socialize, have a chat, and most of all to whet the appetite for dinner.

1 oz	Cloudberry Gin
¾ oz	Campari
¾ oz	sweet vermouth
2 oz	club soda
2–3	dashes of Cloudberry Bitters
	orange peel, thin strip

Glass: *tall Collins*

Pour gin, Campari, and vermouth over ice in your glass. Top with club soda and stir. Add bitters. Singe orange peel, then give a gentle squeeze of the edges over the drink to release the oils. Pop it into the drink, sit back, and enjoy.

LAST WORD

————

The name makes me think this is the last cocktail to have, just getting the last word in and signing off for the night. It is a classic that fell out of fashion in the 1920s. Prohibition in the United States probably helped send it to obscurity, but, thankfully, it has returned with the cocktail renaissance.

The complex Chartreuse, with over 130 herbs and spices, blends with the botanicals of the gin to create a superb base. By adding the cherry liqueur, and lime juice to lift it up, you have a refined, unique cocktail that constantly reveals new flavour profiles as you sip.

¾ oz	Seaweed Gin
¾ oz	cherry liqueur
¾ oz	green Chartreuse
¾ oz	freshly squeezed lime juice
dash	bitters

Glass: *coupe*

Place all ingredients in cocktail shaker with ice. Shake. Strain into coupe. Add bitters and enjoy.

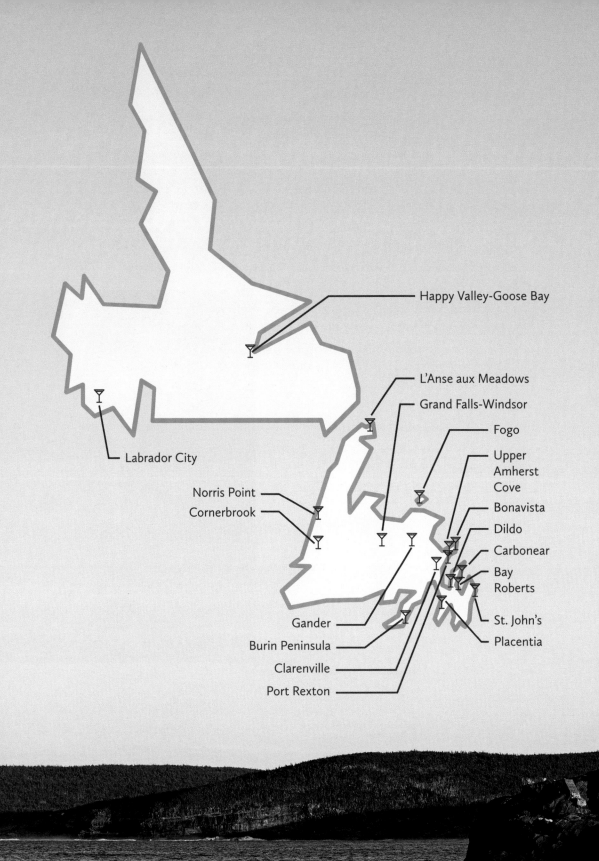

Happy Valley-Goose Bay

L'Anse aux Meadows

Grand Falls-Windsor

Fogo

Upper
Amherst
Cove

Bonavista

Dildo

Carbonear

Bay
Roberts

St. John's

Placentia

Labrador City

Norris Point

Cornerbrook

Gander

Burin Peninsula

Clarenville

Port Rexton

COCKTAILS FROM NEWFOUNDLAND AND LABRADOR BARS, BREWERIES, AND RESTAURANTS

W e are immensely fortunate to have an extraordinary array of fantastic bars, breweries, and restaurants across the province. Many of them are award winning, several are nationally and internationally renowned, and almost all use locally produced, grown, and foraged ingredients.

They all have the art of a good cocktail in common. We've been incredibly lucky to work with them and feel very honoured they have chosen to use our spirits for some of their cocktails. We hope you have fun trying their cocktails and also visiting as many of these wonderful bars, breweries, and restaurants that you can.

The martini glass icons illustrate the locations of all the bars, breweries, and restaurants that have contributed a recipe to this book. This is an easy visual reference for anyone wanting to have a "cocktail tour" of the province.

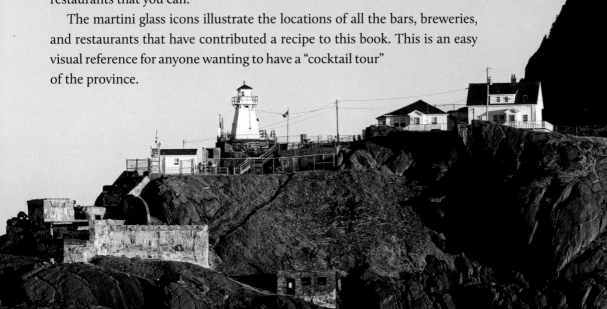

BARS, BREWERIES, AND RESTAURANTS AND THEIR COCKTAILS

ST. JOHN'S

THE THIRD PLACE COCKTAIL CO.
Cuba Libre / Milanese G&T /
Elderflower Fizz

CHINCHED
Lychee and Cassis Italian Soda /
Rose 75

MALLARD COTTAGE
Pfefferling / Golden Hour

THE MERCHANT TAVERN
Blueberry Buckle / Bulldog /
Cucumber Reviver / Homegrown

TERRE
Vital Friend / The Pen Pal

LIV
Coral Green / Corsage

EVOO
Cloud 9

LOOSE TIE
The Loose Tie

GYPSY TEA ROOM
Raspberry Basil Mojito /
Espresso Martini

BREWDOCK
Dock Daiquiri / Seaweed Gin Gimlet

NO. 4
Gin Gatsby / Capsize

ST. JOHN'S FISH EXCHANGE
Sprung Greenhouse

WATERWEST
Dry Dock / Red Stratus

BAY ROBERTS
BACCALIEU TRAIL
BREWING COMPANY
English Morning

CARBONEAR
DARKSTAR COFFEE ROASTERS
Dark Star Espresso Martin /
Dark Hour Sour

COLDWATER FOODS & CAFÉ
Esteban / Pink Lady

DILDO
DILDO BREWING
COMPANY & MUSEUM
Mai Dildo Beer

PLACENTIA
THREE SISTERS
East Coast Slammer /
Right Red 'And /
Clarke's Beach Iced Tea

CLARENVILLE
BELLA'S CASUAL DINING
"Get Baked" Cider Cocktail /
Après-ski

PORT REXTON
FISHERS' LOFT
Partridgeberry Martini

BONAVISTA
RAGGED ROCKS GASTROPUB
Partridgeberry Sour / A Sip Above

UPPER AMHERST COVE
BONAVISTA SOCIAL CLUB
Rhubarb Lemonade

GANDER
THE NEWFOUNDLAND TEA CO.
Raspberry Lemonade Mar-TEA-ni /
Rhubarb Berry Fizz /
Island Time Latte

FOGO
FOGO ISLAND INN
L. L. / Cloudberry Birch
Old Fashioned

BANGBELLY CAFÉ
All-Day Breakfast /
Lemon Meringue Tart

BURIN PENINSULA
SMUGGLERS COVE ROADHOUSE
PATIO-BAR & GRILL
It's Blueberry Thyme /
Smugglers' Harvest

LABRADOR CITY
BABA Q'S SMOKE & GRILL
Heavenly Cloudberry /
RhuBABA Jam Jam /
Midnight Haze

HAPPY VALLEY-GOOSE BAY
MAXWELL'S NIGHTCLUB
Rhubarb Martini /
Cloudberry Cocktail

GRAND FALLS-WINDSOR
LEFTY'S PIZZERIA
Seaweed Sunrise /
Scandinavian Sweet and Sour

NORRIS POINT
THE BLACK SPRUCE RESTAURANT
Cloudberry Cosmo /
Gin and Sage Mule

L'ANSE AUX MEADOWS
THE NORSEMAN RESTAURANT
Rhubarb Fizz

CORNER BROOK
BOOTLEG BREW CO.
Lemon Meringue Sour /
Chaga Nog

BEST COAST RESTAURANT
Blue Man: A Tea /
Shake and Bakeapple

THE THIRD PLACE COCKTAIL CO.

These folks make specialty tonics and shrubs, by hand, in small batches, in St. John's. *(Photos: Matthew Wells, Georgetown Cocktail Club)*

CUBA LIBRE

2 oz	Gunpowder & Rose Rum
1 oz	The Third Place Cocktail Co. Kola
2 oz	fizzy water
½ oz	freshly squeezed lime juice
	lime wedge, fresh mint,
	for garnish

Glass: *Collins*

Build in the glass over ice and stir until incorporated and chilled. Garnish with a lime wedge and fresh mint bouquet.

MILANESE G&T

1 oz	Cloudberry Gin
1 oz	Italian red bitter liqueur
1 oz	The Third Place Cocktail Co. Tonic
2–3	dashes of Cloudberry Bitters
2 oz	fizzy water
	orange wedge, for garnish

Glass: Collins

Build in the glass over ice and stir until just
incorporated and chilled. Top with fizzy water and
garnish with an orange wedge.

ELDERFLOWER FIZZ

1 oz	vodka
½ oz	The Third Place Cocktail Co. Elderflower
½ oz	freshly squeezed lemon juice
¼ oz	orgeat (sweet syrup)
2–3 oz	sparkling wine
	thin strip of lemon peel, for garnish

Glass: flute

In a cocktail shaker, combine vodka, elderflower, juice,
and orgeat. Add ice and shake until well chilled. Fine
strain into a flute and top with sparkling wine. Twist
the lemon strip and use as garnish.

CHINCHED

———

From downtown St. John's, Chinched restaurant produces all of their own charcuterie and other meats. *(Cocktails and photos: Danny Vin Le)*

LYCHEE AND CASSIS ITALIAN SODA

¾ oz	crème de cassis
1 oz	lychee syrup
¼ oz	SOHO lychee liqueur
¾ oz	lime juice
1 oz	Newfoundland Distillery Co. Vodka
	lime slice, for garnish

Glass: Collins

Pour crème de cassis into bottom of shaker. Fill with ice and shake. Pour over ice in your glass, stir in other ingredients, and garnish.

ROSE 75

¾ oz	rose petal syrup	1 oz	Prosecco
¾ oz	lemon juice		rose petals,
1 oz	Cloudberry Gin		for garnish

Glass: flute

Shake syrup, juice, and gin together. Pour into flute, top with Prosecco, stir gently, and garnish.

MALLARD COTTAGE

In an old heritage building in Quidi Vidi, Mallard Cottage is one of the top restaurants in the province. Their menu showcases local ingredients.

PFEFFERLING

1 ½ oz	Chaga Rum	1 oz	egg white
½ oz	red vermouth	2–3	dashes of Chaga &
⅔ oz	mushroom-maple		Chanterelle Bitters
	simple syrup		nutmeg, for garnish
½ oz	lime juice		

Glass: coupe

Dry shake all ingredients for about 30 seconds, then add ice and shake again for 30 seconds. Strain through a fine-mesh strainer into your glass. Garnish with nutmeg.

GOLDEN HOUR

1 ½ oz	Cloudberry Gin	½ oz	yellow Chartreuse
½ oz	verjus (*sour grape juice*)		edible flower,
½ oz	dry vermouth		for garnish

Glass: coupe

Put all ingredients into a glass mixing jar with ice and stir for 30 seconds or until cold. Strain into your glass and garnish with an edible flower.

THE MERCHANT TAVERN

Another top restaurant, in an old bank in downtown St. John's, that uses fresh local produce and serves a wide array of wines and cocktails.

BLUEBERRY BUCKLE

1 ½ oz	Cloudberry Gin
¾ oz	lemon juice
¾ oz	St. Germain
1 oz	blueberry syrup
	club soda, for top-up

Glass: Collins

Pour ingredients other than club soda in shaker, shake, pour into glass, top with soda.

BULLDOG

1 ½ oz	Seaweed Gin
1 oz	cranberry juice
1 oz	grapefruit juice
½ oz	honey
	Prosecco, for top-up

Glass: coupe

Pour ingredients other than Prosecco in shaker, shake, pour into glass, top with Prosecco.

HOMEGROWN

1 ½ oz	Seaweed Gin
3/4 oz	egg whites
½ oz	St. Germain
3/4 oz	lemon juice
½ oz	Irish Mist
½ oz	honey
4 drops	bitters, for garnish

Glass: coupe

Dry shake, then shake with ice, strain into coupe, garnish, and serve.

CUCUMBER REVIVER

1 slice	cucumber
1 oz	club soda, plus some for top-up
½ oz	Aperol
½ oz	Newfoundland Distillery Co. Vodka
½ oz	lime juice
3/4 oz	simple syrup

Glass: coupe

Muddle cucumber with club soda. Pour Aperol, vodka, lime juice, and simple syrup in shaker, shake, pour into glass, top with club soda.

TERRE

Located in the Alt Hotel, Terre won best hotel restaurant in Canada in 2021. Terre uses local produce in innovative ways.

VITAL FRIEND *(Photo and recipe: Michael Sheppard, bartender, and owner of Ouishep cocktail catering)*

For the dill-infused vermouth

5 oz	extra-dry vermouth, preferably Noilly Prat
1 tbsp	dried dill

For the cocktail

1 oz	dill-infused vermouth
1 ½ oz	Aquavit
1 oz	Italian-style red bitter
2	dashes of Sweet Gale & Rose Bitters
	sprig fresh dillweed, for garnish

Glass: *cocktail*

For vermouth, put dried dill and vermouth in a 150 ml container, seal, and shake well. Refrigerate for at least six hours or overnight. Using cheesecloth or a coffee filter rinsed with hot water, strain the liquid and keep in a sealed container in the fridge for up to two weeks.

For cocktail, combine all ingredients in a stirring glass, except the garnish. Add lots of ice and stir briefly until well chilled and diluted to about 4 ½ ounces. Strain into chilled glass; garnish with dillweed. Enjoy immediately, preferably with soft cheeses and preserves, before or after dinner.

THE PEN PAL *(Alexi Ladéroute, photo: Matthew Wells)*

1 ½ oz   Gunpower & Rose Rum

½ oz   cognac

½ oz   amaro (Amaro Montenegro preferred)

⅓ oz   port (10-year-old Taylor preferred)

2   dashes of Chaga & Chanterelle Bitters

Glass: *coupe*

Mix all ingredients over ice in mixing glass. Stir for 20 seconds. Strain into coupe. Add bitters.

DEEP DO-ALL BITTERS

3 parts   Cloudberry Bitters

1 part   Chanterelle & Chaga Bitters

2 parts   aromatic bitters

Combine in a dasher bottle to enhance any cocktail driven by aged (non-clear) spirits.

ZESTY DO-ALL BITTERS

2 parts   Cloudberry Bitters

1 part   Seaweed Bitters

1 part   orange bitters

Combine in a dasher bottle to enhance any spirit-forward clear cocktail, especially martinis.

LIV

On Water Street in St. John's, featuring Asian fusion food and wide range of cocktails. (*Photos: Margarita Kusaikina*)

CORAL GREEN (*Johnathan Schwartz*)

1 ½ oz	Seaweed Gin
1 oz	blue Curaçao
1 ½ oz	pineapple juice
	fresh mint leaves, for garnish

Glass: *rocks*

Put ice in cocktail shaker. Add all ingredients and shake for 20 seconds. Strain, serve, and garnish.

CORSAGE (*Greg Savage*)

2 oz	Gunpowder & Rose Rum
1 oz	lime juice
1 oz	rose petal syrup
	rose petal, for garnish

Glass: *coupe*

Put ice in cocktail shaker. Add all ingredients and shake for 20 seconds. Strain, serve, and garnish.

EVOO

In the Murray Premises, just off Water Street, with Mediterranean-influenced food, wine, and cocktails. (*Photos: Margarita Kusaikina*)

CLOUD 9

1 ½ oz	Cloudberry Gin
½ oz	Cointreau
½ oz	Galliano
½ oz	simple syrup
⅓ oz	lemon juice
1 oz	orange juice
1	egg white
	¼ slice of orange, for garnish

Glass: Collins

Dry shake (no ice) all ingredients for 15 seconds in a cocktail shaker. Add ice and shake for 15 more seconds. Strain over ice in a glass and garnish.

LOOSE TIE

A late-night spot just above George Street focusing on cocktails, with food and drinks too.

THE LOOSE TIE

1 oz	Chaga Rum
1 oz	St. Germain
	juice of 1 lemon
½ oz	maple syrup
	club soda, as top-up

Glass: Collins

Shake first four ingredients on ice. Top with soda.

GYPSY TEA ROOM

In the historic Murray Premises, this tea room mixes classic drinks and modern food with great creativity.

RASPBERRY BASIL MOJITO

½ oz	lime juice, freshly squeezed	1 oz	Gunpowder & Rose Rum
5	raspberries	½ oz	Chambord
1 oz	simple syrup		fresh basil leaf,
3	basil leaves		for garnish

Glass: stemless wine glass

Combine lime, raspberries, syrup, and basil, and muddle in a shaker. Add other ingredients and shake with ice. Strain over new ice in your glass and garnish.

ESPRESSO MARTINI

1 oz	vodka	1 oz	espresso
½ oz	Cabot Trail Maple Cream	3	coffee beans, for garnish
½ oz	Kahlua		

Glass: coupe

Combine all ingredients in a shaker with ice. Strain into glass and garnish.

They have over twenty-four different types of beer on tap, as well as cocktails and contemporary food.

DOCK DAIQUIRI

2 oz	Gunpowder & Rose Rum
2 oz	freshly squeezed lime juice
1 oz	simple syrup
	cranberry, for garnish

Glass: rocks

Shake all ingredients on ice. Strain into sugar-rimmed glass of ice. Top with cranberry, don't stir.

SEAWEED GIN GIMLET

2 oz	Seaweed or Cloudberry Gin
1 ½ oz	simple syrup
1 oz	freshly squeezed lime juice
3-4	dashes of Seaweed & Nettle Bitters
	lime slice, for garnish

Glass: rocks

Shake on ice. Strain into glass full of ice and garnish.

Opposite the Anglican Cathedral in downtown St. John's, an old-school bar with cocktails and locally sourced food.

GIN GATSBY (*Hilarie Vatcher*)

	rose petal sugar, to rim	½ oz	agave syrup
1 ½ oz	Seaweed Gin	¾ oz	lime juice
½ oz	St. Germain		lime flower, for garnish
1 oz	pure cranberry juice		

Glass: *cosmo*

Rim glass with sugar. Put ice in shaker, shake all ingredients, fine strain, pour into chilled glass, add garnish.

CAPSIZE (*Michael Billard*)

1 ½ oz	Gunpowder & Rose Rum
¾ oz	agave syrup
¾ oz	lime juice
4	fresh basil leaves
2	dashes of Newfoundland Distillery Classic Bitters Prosecco, for top-up

Glass: *small coupe*

Combine all ingredients except Prosecco and one basil leaf in a shaker. Muddle basil, fine strain in glass, and top with Prosecco. Garnish with remaining basil leaf.

ST. JOHN'S FISH EXCHANGE

The Fish Exchange has great views over the harbour, focusing, naturally, on fish, with other crowd-pleasers and cocktails.

SPRUNG GREENHOUSE

	sprinkle sugar
	sprinkle dried cilantro
	cucumber slice
	small piece fresh ginger
1 ½ oz	simple syrup
1 ½ oz	Seaweed Gin
½ oz	lime juice
3	cucumber slices, for garnish

Glass: *rocks*

Combine sugar and dried cilantro, rim your glass with it, and fill with ice. Muddle cucumber slice and fresh ginger in shaker, fill with ice, add liquid ingredients, and shake. Pour into glass and garnish.

WATERWEST

Above a traditional butcher shop in St. John's, with an in-store deli specializing in freshly made foods, including pasta. Also serve wines and cocktails.

DRY DOCK *(George Ingerman)*

1 oz	Chaga Rum	¾ oz	pineapple syrup
1 oz	Aquavit	½ oz	freshly squeezed
¾ oz	Aperol		lime juice
½ oz	sweet vermouth		

dehydrated lime, pineapple, for garnish

Glass: goblet

Mix ingredients with crushed ice, shake, and pour into glass. Garnish.

RED STRATUS *(Benjamin Davis)*

10	raspberries	2 oz	Cloudberry Gin
6	basil leaves, to	¾ oz	lemon
	muddle	¾ oz	lime
4	cucumber slices	¾ oz	honey syrup

tonic water, for top-up (Fever-Tree preferred)
fresh basil leaf, cucumber slice, for garnish

Glass: rocks

Muddle raspberries, basil, and cucumber. Shake with gin, juices, and syrup, and double strain. Top up with tonic. Garnish with cucumber and basil.

BACCALIEU TRAIL BREWING COMPANY

A microbrewery right on the ocean in Bay Roberts, serving a full range of beer and cocktails, and some food.

ENGLISH MORNING

2 oz	Cloudberry Gin
½ oz	simple syrup
6 oz	grapefruit juice
5	fresh basil leaves

Glass: rocks

Add gin, syrup, and grapefruit juice to a cocktail shaker with several ice cubes. Smack three or four basil leaves between your hands to release essential oils, give them a rough tear, and add to shaker. Shake vigorously, then serve over ice, and garnish with remaining basil leaf.

DARKSTAR COFFEE ROASTERS

Carbonear's only coffee roaster. They also make their own food and serve cocktails.

DARK STAR ESPRESSO MARTINI

2 oz	Seaweed Gin
1 ½ oz	Dark Star Espresso
½ oz	simple syrup
3	espresso beans, for garnish

Glass: martini

Combine all ingredients in a shaker over ice. Vigorously shake for 20 seconds and strain into the glass. Spoon remaining foam on top, if desired, and garnish.

DARK HOUR SOUR

2 oz	Chaga Rum
2 oz	cold-brew coffee
1 oz	brown sugar simple syrup
	juice of ½ lemon
	lemon zest, for garnish

Glass: rocks

Pour rum into your glass over ice and add coffee, syrup, and lemon juice. Stir and garnish with lemon zest.

Located on Water Street in Carbonear, a bar and restaurant using local produce and adding a little international flair.

ESTEBAN

1 oz	Chaga Rum
1 oz	pineapple juice
	ginger ale, for top-up
	lime slice, for garnish

Glass: rocks

Place ice in glass. Add Chaga Rum and pineapple juice. Top with ginger ale and garnish.

PINK LADY

1 oz	Rhubarb Vodka
2 oz	rhubarb syrup
¼ oz	lemon juice
¼ oz	lime juice
	lemon slice, for garnish

Glass: coupe

Put ice in cocktail shaker. Add all ingredients. Shake. Rim glass with sugar. Pour. Garnish with a lemon slice.

DILDO BREWING COMPANY & MUSEUM

Overlooking Dildo harbour, they make their own beer, operate a full restaurant, and even have a museum downstairs.

MAI DILDO BEER

8 oz   Dildo Lager
1 oz   Chaga Rum
1 oz   simple syrup
        juice of ½ lime, freshly squeezed
        rosemary sprig, lime or pineapple wedge,
            for garnish

Glass: beer or pint glass

Combine beer with rum, simple syrup, and lime juice. Serve on lots of ice and garnish.

THREE SISTERS

On the mouth of the narrows in Placentia, a full bar and restaurant serving local food and drinks, often with their own twist.

EAST COAST SLAMMER

¾ oz	Rhubarb Flavoured Vodka
¾ oz	Cloudberry Gin
½ oz	Amaro Montenegro
1 ½ oz	Purity orange syrup
2 oz	Nova 7 sparkling wine or club soda
1 tsp	grenadine, orange zest, for garnish

Glass: highball

Pour vodka, gin, and amaro into your glass. Add ice and pour syrup over it. Top with wine or club soda. Finish with grenadine and orange zest.

RIGHT RED 'AND

1 ½ oz	Gunpowder & Rose Rum
¾ oz	Aperol
¾ oz	sweet vermouth (Dolin preferred)
2	dashes of Chaga & Chanterelle Bitters, for garnish

Glass: coupe

Into a mixing glass, pour rum, Aperol, and vermouth. Add ice to glass, stir until glass is cold, strain into coupe. Garnish with bitters.

CLARKE'S BEACH ICED TEA

½ oz	Chaga Rum
½ oz	Cloudberry Gin
½ oz	Rhubarb Vodka
½ oz	Aquavit
½ oz	Triple Sec
1 oz	lemon juice
½ oz	tea simple syrup
2 oz	club soda, for top-up

Glass: pint

Mix all ingredients except club soda in your glass, add ice, and top up with soda.

BELLA'S CASUAL DINING

In Clarenville, serving a range of local favourites, with daily specials and cocktails.

"GET BAKED" CIDER COCKTAIL (*Susan Godfrey*)

1 ½ oz	Cloudberry Gin
5 oz	Forager Apple Cider
4–5	shakes of Cloudberry Bitters
3	bakeapple berries, for garnish
3	apple slices, thin like a fan, for garnish

Glass: *stemless wineglass*

Add lots of ice to your glass, pour ingredients over ice, mix, then garnish with apple slices and bakeapples.

APRÈS-SKI *(Susan Godfrey)*

For Aquavit-infused chocolate mousse

4 ½ oz	dark chocolate
1 tbsp	unsalted butter
3	fresh eggs, separated
2 tsp	confectioner's sugar
4 oz	whipped cream, plus some for garnish
½ oz	Aquavit
2 tbsp	strong coffee, cooled

For cocktail

4 oz	strong coffee or double espresso, cooled
1 oz	Aquavit
	dollop chocolate mousse, for garnish
	3 coffee beans, for garnish

Glass: *coupe*

For mousse, shave some chocolate and save for garnish. Melt remaining chocolate with butter and set aside. Beat egg whites and half of the sugar to form soft peaks and set aside. Whisk yolks with remaining sugar until thick, set aside. Mix Aquavit and coffee and set aside. In a medium chilled glass or steel bowl, fold together chocolate mixture and whipped cream, then fold in Aquavit and coffee. Fold in egg whites until colour is consistent. Do not over-mix. Store in fridge.

For cocktail, mix coffee and Aquavit. Garnish with chocolate mousse, whipped cream, coffee beans, and reserved chocolate shavings.

FISHERS' LOFT

At Port Rexton's Fishers' Loft Inn, the dining room overlooks the bay and has set menus inspired by the garden and sea.

PARTRIDGEBERRY MARTINI

1 ½ oz	The Newfoundland Distillery Co. Vodka
¾ oz	Cointreau
¾ oz	freshly squeezed lime juice
1 oz	white cranberry juice
¼ oz	partridgeberry coulis
	partridgeberries and/or orange zest, for garnish

Glass: *chilled martini*

Combine vodka, Cointreau, lime juice, cranberry juice, and partridgeberry coulis in a cocktail shaker with ice and shake until well chilled. Strain into chilled glass and garnish.

RAGGED ROCKS GASTROPUB

You'll find Ragged Rocks in Bonavista offering local spirits and fine dining.
(*Photos: Rodney and Sonya Gray*)

PARTRIDGEBERRY SOUR

1 oz	egg white
2 oz	Aquavit
1 oz	lime juice
1 oz	simple syrup
1 ½ tbsp	partridgeberry jam
	lime slice, for garnish

Glass: *rocks*

Dry shake egg white in cocktail shaker (without ice). Add Aquavit, lime juice, simple syrup, and jam with ice to shaker and shake well. Using strainer, pour mixture into your glass over ice, and garnish.

A SIP ABOVE

2 oz	Rhubarb Vodka
	cranberry mango juice
	lemon slice, for garnish

Glass: *goblet*

Mix and serve over ice.

BONAVISTA SOCIAL CLUB

With a wood-fired bread oven at its centre, this Upper Amherst Cove restaurant uses local game and fish in season, as well as vegetables from their garden. (*Photo is moose burger and house-made potato chips, served with partridgeberry ketchup, roasted garlic aioli, and coleslaw.*)

RHUBARB LEMONADE

2 parts	stewed rhubarb	1 part	simple syrup
1 part	lemon juice	1 oz	Seaweed Gin

Glass: *8 oz*

Stew the rhubarb until the stalks are reduced to pulp. Strain and cool, mix with juice and syrup to make the lemonade. To serve, put ice in your glass, pour in gin, and top with rhubarb lemonade.

THE NEWFOUNDLAND TEA CO.

A tea company in Gander that is also a contemporary restaurant serving classic foods with a twist.

RHUBARB BERRY FIZZ

For peppercorn simple syrup:

1½ cups	water
2 tbsp	whole peppercorns
1 cup	sugar

For cocktail:

1½ oz	Rhubarb Vodka
3 oz	Newfoundland Tea Co. Berry Burst tea, chilled
¾ oz	peppercorn simple syrup
¾ oz	lime juice, freshly squeezed
	sparkling water, for top-up
	rosemary sprig, lime slice, strawberry, for garnish

Glass: *rocks*

To make syrup, simmer water with peppercorns for about 10 minutes. Strain to remove peppercorns and discard. Return remaining infusion to simmer, add sugar, simmer until slightly thickened, about 2 minutes.

To make cocktail, shake everything but water with ice. Pour into glass over fresh ice. Top with sparkling water, garnish.

RASPBERRY LEMONADE MAR-TEA-NI

1½ oz   Cloudberry Gin

3   dashes of Sweet Gale & Wild Rose Bitters

2 oz   Newfoundland Tea Co. Raspberry
            Lemonade tea, chilled

¾ oz   honey simple syrup
            sugar, for glass rim
            lemon slice, for garnish

Glass: *martini*

Shake all ingredients with ice. Rim glass with lemon. Dip glass into sugar, so it's around the rim. Pour drink, garnish.

ISLAND TIME LATTE

3 oz   Newfoundland Tea Co. Cinnamon
            Chai tea, hot

1 ½ oz Gunpowder & Rose Rum

1 tsp   sugar, or to taste

3 oz   steamed coconut milk (ideally from
            a carton and not canned)
            cinnamon stick, for garnish

Glass: *Collins*

Steep tea until extra strong. Add rum and sugar, and stir until sugar is dissolved. Pour in steamed coconut milk. Garnish and enjoy hot.

FOGO ISLAND INN

The restaurant and bar at the Inn, perched above the shoreline, welcomes all and concentrates on local produce.

L. L.

1 ½ oz	Seaweed Gin		1	egg white
½ oz	green Chartreuse		1 oz	lilac simple syrup
1 oz	lemon juice			
3	dashes of Peychaud's Bitters, for garnish			

Glass: *coupe*

Pour everything except bitters into cocktail shaker with no ice. Shake hard until frothy/creamy. Add ice to shaker and shake vigorously for 20 seconds. Double strain over glass and garnish with bitters.

CLOUDBERRY BIRCH OLD FASHIONED

	lemon rind
5	dashes of Cloudberry Bitters
1 oz	simple syrup
2 oz	Cloudberry Gin
	small strip birchbark
	bakeapples, for garnish

Glass: *coupe*

Place lemon rind, bitters, and syrup in bottom of mixing glass. Muddle well. Pour gin over. Add ice. Stir/taste until desired dilution is achieved. Meanwhile, light birch bark with a smoke gun, and capture smoke under your glass. Invert smoky glass and pour drink into it. Add a large ice cube and garnish.

BANGBELLY CAFÉ

In Fogo, fresh seasonal food all made from scratch, with proper coffee, cocktails, and wines too.

LEMON MERINGUE TART

For vanilla simple syrup

1 cup	water
1 cup	turbinado or raw sugar
1 tsp	vanilla extract

For cocktail

2 oz	The Newfoundland Distillery Co. Vodka (or Rhubarb Vodka for a flavourful twist)
1 oz	lemon juice
¾ oz	vanilla simple syrup
1	egg white (or ¾–1 oz aquafaba)
1	dash of bitters
	meringue cookie crumbs, to rim
	candied lemon peel, for garnish

Glass: coupe

For syrup, combine water and sugar in a small pot and bring to a boil, then remove from heat. Stir in the vanilla extract.

For cocktail, in a chilled cocktail shaker, combine vodka, lemon juice, syrup, and egg white. Shake vigorously until frothy. Brush rim with lemon, then rim glass with crushed meringue, strain drink into it, add bitters and garnish.

ALL-DAY BREAKFAST

For toast simple syrup:

¼ cup	steel-cut oats
1 cup	water
1 cup	raw sugar

For candied bacon:

	bacon, amount preferred
1 tsp	brown sugar per slice of bacon

For cocktail:

2 oz	Aquavit
½ oz	toast simple syrup
2 oz	freshly squeezed orange juice
1	fresh egg white (or ¾–1 oz aquafaba—water left from boiled chickpeas)
	toasted breadcrumbs, to rim glass
2	dashes of bitters
1 slice	candied bacon, for garnish
1 slice	navel orange, for garnish

For syrup, in a dry pan over medium-high heat, toast oats until golden brown and fragrant. Combine water and sugar in a saucepan and bring to a boil, then remove from heat. Steep the oats in syrup for 10 minutes, and then strain.

For candied bacon, on a parchment-lined baking sheet, par cook bacon for 10 minutes at 400° F; remove from oven, drain grease and toss bacon with brown sugar. Return it to a clean baking sheet lined with parchment, placing a second sheet of parchment and another clean baking sheet on top. Bake for 5 to 10 minutes, until caramelized. Transfer to rack to cool and crisp. (Bacon can be refrigerated, wrapped in wax paper in an airtight container, for up to 3 weeks.)

In a dry cocktail shaker, combine Aquavit, syrup, and orange juice. Stir to combine. Add egg white; shake vigorously until frothy. Rub orange slice on rim of glass, then rim your glass with breadcrumbs, strain cocktail over ice into it, add bitters, and garnish.

SMUGGLERS COVE ROADHOUSE
PATIO-BAR & GRILL

Pub and grill in Burin with all the classics and cocktails too.

IT'S BLUEBERRY THYME

For blueberry simple syrup

1 cup   sugar

1 cup   water

1 cup   wild blueberries (Walsh's Farm)

4   sprigs fresh thyme

For cocktail

1 ½ oz   Seaweed Gin

¾ oz   lime juice

1 ¼ oz   blueberry simple syrup

          bitter lemon soda, for top-up

          lime wedge, thyme sprig, for garnish

Glass: cocktail

For syrup, combine all ingredients in a pot and bring to a boil. Reduce to simmer and continue for 10 minutes. Let cool overnight. Strain syrup into bottle while squeezing blueberries to retain their juice. Add gin, lime juice, and syrup to a cocktail shaker with ice and shake. Strain into cocktail glass over ice. Top with bitter lemon soda. Garnish.

SMUGGLERS' HARVEST

For a large batch of spiced simple syrup

2 cups	water
1 cup	white sugar
1 cup	dark brown sugar
1 ½ tsp	vanilla extract
1 tsp	allspice
3	cinnamon sticks

For cocktail

1 ¾ oz	Chaga Rum
1 ½ oz	pure apple cider
1 ½ oz	spiced simple syrup
½ oz	lemon juice
	ginger beer, for top-up
	cinnamon stick and/or apple slice, for garnish.

Glass: *cocktail*

For syrup, mix all ingredients in a pot and bring to a boil. Reduce to simmer and continue for 10 minutes. Let cool overnight. Discard cinnamon sticks and strain syrup into bottle.

Pour rum, cider, syrup, and lemon juice into a cocktail shaker with ice and shake. Strain into glass over ice. Top with ginger beer. Garnish.

BABA Q'S SMOKE AND GRILL

A traditional smokehouse with a modern twist—and cocktails—in Labrador City.

HEAVENLY CLOUDBERRY

1 oz	Cloudberry Gin
½ oz	Cointreau
2 oz	freshly squeezed orange juice
½ oz	freshly squeezed lemon juice
4–6	fresh mint leaves
	berries, for garnish

Glass: highball

Shake all on ice and strain into your glass over fresh ice. Garnish.

RHUBABA JAM JAM

1 ½ oz	Rhubarb Vodka
½ oz	peach schnapps
2 oz	pineapple juice
½ oz	pomegranate syrup
	club soda, for top-up
	pineapple slice, pomegranate seeds, rosemary sprigs, for garnish

Glass: *stemless wineglass*

Shake vodka, schnapps, and juice on ice and strain. Pour into glass over fresh ice. Add syrup and top with soda. Garnish.

MIDNIGHT HAZE

1 ½ oz	Chaga Rum
½ oz	Martini Rosso
½ oz	ginger syrup
½ oz	each freshly squeezed lemon, lime, orange juice
	dehydrated orange slice, cinnamon stick, for garnish

Glass: *rocks*

Shake all ingredients with ice, then strain and pour over a large block of ice. Garnish.

MAXWELL'S NIGHTCLUB

Maxwell's is in the same thirty-five-year-old establishment as Bentley's Restaurant in Happy Valley-Goose Bay.

RHUBARB MARTINI

2 oz	Rhubarb Vodka
2 oz	pineapple juice
3–4	drops of grenadine

Glass: *martini*

Shake vodka and juice over ice, strain into glass, top with grenadine.

CLOUDBERRY COCKTAIL

1 oz	Cloudberry Gin
1 oz	Galliano
1 oz	pineapple juice
dash	grenadine
	orange slice, for garnish

Glass: *hurricane*

Put ice in glass. Add all ingredients, stir, and garnish.

LEFTY'S PIZZERIA

A family-owned pizza restaurant and bar that has been going for thirty-five years in Grand Falls-Windsor. (*Photos: Adrian and Tyler Whiffen*)

SEAWEED SUNRISE (*Adrian and Tyler Whiffen*)

1 oz	Seaweed Gin
¾ oz	pineapple juice
¼ oz	7up
1 tsp	Purity Raspberry Syrup
	pineapple slice, for garnish

Glass: *goblet*

Fill glass to top with ice. Add gin, juice, and 7up. Finish with syrup. Garnish. Stir before sipping.

SCANDINAVIAN SWEET AND SOUR

(*Adrian and Tyler Whiffen*)

2 oz	lime cordial	⅔ oz	pineapple juice
1 oz	Aquavit		lime slice, for garnish
⅓ oz	orange juice		

Glass: *goblet*

Fill glass with ice. Shake pineapple vigorously for froth. Add ingredients in order listed, for the colour pattern. Garnish. Stir before sipping.

THE BLACK SPRUCE RESTAURANT

In Neddies Harbour Inn boutique hotel in Gros Morne National Park, the Black Spruce is dedicated to using locally produced food and products. (*Photos: Beatrice Stutz and Jason Lynch*)

CLOUDBERRY COSMO (*Beatrice Stutz, Jason Lynch*)

2 oz	Cloudberry Gin
½ oz	freshly squeezed lemon juice
½ oz	simple syrup
1 tsp	partridgeberry preserves

Glass: *coupe*

Combine all ingredients in cocktail shaker, fill with ice, shake until chilled (about 15 seconds), strain into glass.

GIN AND SAGE MULE

(*Beatrice Stutz, Jason Lynch*)

2 oz	Seaweed Gin
½ oz	freshly squeezed lime juice
	ginger beer, for top-up
	twig fresh sage or mint, for garnish

Glass: *ideally a copper mug, but rocks will do*

Fill cup with ice, add gin and lime juice, top with ginger beer, and garnish.

NORSEMAN RESTAURANT

In L'Anse aux Meadows, with superb views, local seafood, wild game, wine, and cocktails.

RHUBARB FIZZ

1 oz	rhubarb concentrate
2 oz	gin
½ oz	simple syrup
	soda water, for top-up
	lemon wedge, for garnish

Glass: stemless wineglass

Put ice in mixing glass. Add rhubarb concentrate, gin, and syrup, and stir for 15 seconds. Strain over ice. Top up with club soda. Garnish.

Small-batch craft brewery in downtown Corner Brook, serves beer, cocktails, and charcuterie.

LEMON MERINGUE SOUR

2 oz	Seaweed Gin
1 oz	freshly squeezed lemon juice
¾ oz	vanilla syrup
1	egg white
¼ oz	olive oil
	lemon strip, thinly sliced

Glass: 8-oz cocktail of your preference

Fill glass with ice to chill. Add all ingredients to cocktail shaker, or Mason jar, making sure to add the egg white last and right before shaking. Don't let the egg sit with the citrus juice for too long, as it will not get fluffy.

Dry shake (without ice) in a shaker or jar. Open after the first few shakes to release some of the building pressure from the aerating egg white—and to avoid a possible cocktail explosion!

Continue to shake for 5 to 8 seconds or until the shaker is cold. Strain into glass. Use a peeler to pull a strip of lemon zest and express the oils over the cocktail. Use it as a garnish or drop it right into the glass. Cheers!

CHAGA NOG

This is a staple Christmas cocktail at the Bootleg taproom, but we strongly encourage you to enjoy it on any chilly evening by the wood stove or on the couch, wrapped up in a blanket, indulging in TV.

For coffee syrup

1 cup	boiling water
1 cup	sugar
½ cup	coarse ground coffee

For cocktail

1 ½ oz	Chaga Rum
¼ oz	Drambuie
½ oz	coffee syrup
1	whole raw egg
3 oz	2% or 3.25% milk
	nutmeg, grated, for garnish
	cinnamon, coffee beans, and/or star anise, for additional garnish, if desired

Glass: *10 oz rocks*

For syrup, mix water, sugar, and coffee. Whisk until sugar is dissolved, let stand for 5 minutes, strain. To get rid of all bits of coffee grounds, strain a second time through a coffee filter.

In a shaker or Mason jar, combine all ingredients except the milk. Dry shake for 20 seconds, making sure the egg is fully incorporated. Add ice and wet shake for 5 to 8 seconds, or until chilled. Strain into your glass filled halfway with ice. Top with milk. If there is room in the glass, add more ice. Garnish as desired. A whole star anise is a great topping! Enjoy! *Note: raw eggs are generally safe for people with healthy immune systems.*

BEST COAST RESTAURANT

———

Part of the Boomstick Brewing Co. in the Hew & Draw Hotel in Corner Brook, with contemporary local food and a full range of beer and cocktails.

BLUE MAN: A TEA

1 oz	orange pekoe tea
1 ¾ oz	Cloudberry Gin
½ oz	lemon juice
1 ¼ oz	wild blueberry syrup
	lemon slice, for garnish

Glass: coupe

Make strong tea (2 teabags to a cup of water, steeped 4 minutes). Mix all ingredients, shake with ice, double strain into coupe, and garnish.

SHAKE AND BAKEAPPLE

1 ½ oz	Cloudberry Gin	½ oz	lemon juice
1 ¼ oz	bakeapple syrup		lemon peel, spiralled

Glass: rocks

Shake gin, syrup, and juice with ice, double strain onto fresh ice in your glass. With a channel knife, strip a piece of lemon peel, curl it with your fingers or around a toothpick, and use as garnish.

ACKNOWLEDGEMENTS

It's rare to get a chance to publicly thank people. There are many wonderful people who have helped make this book happen, so I am trying to cover all the bases.

THE BOOK

Everyone at Breakwater Books, especially Claire Wilkshire and Rebecca Rose, who have made writing and producing this book such a delight! A massive thank you to Dave Howells for the fantastic photos and Rhonda Molloy for the magnificent design and layout. Thank you also to the amazing Lisa Moore for her beautiful introduction and to Amara Wilkins for the excellent illustrations. A special thank you to Valerie Mansour for her superb editing skills; she really has refined and elevated every sentence.

COCKTAILS

We've had incredibly talented, kind, and generous staff at the Tasting Room over the years, making and delivering cocktails. Without them, we wouldn't have gone very far. We have also had a few who, once behind the bar, fell into cocktail making or even mixology—like ducks to water—and have been instrumental in helping create the cocktails that we've served in the Tasting

Room and put in this book. Special thanks to Marek Nakonieczny, Rebecca Webber, Brian Pisani, Kevin Hans, Erin Reynolds, and Kyle Downey.

THE DISTILLERY

Without William Carter, the distillery and this book would not exist. Bill is the magician who has made all the spirits and flavours come to life. It is his knowledge and skill that have enabled us to produce all of our spirits. He has had fantastic help from David Bennett, and they are now producing more spirits than ever and laying down whisky. A profound thank you.

Read, Andrew, and Christopher, have been essential in the set-up and running of the distillery. Thank you for your dedication, diligence, experience, and patience. The office oversees everything and ensures we keep up with all the projects. It's a bit like herding cats, so a very big thank you to Ted Rogers and Kaila LeDrew for their persistence, humour, and fine work. Thanks also to Eve Lynch and Jackie Laracy for keeping the wheels turning, and a special thank you to Ken for watching over all things.

Rock Spirits, who do all of our bottling and final testing of our spirits, are fantastic partners and have a superb team who have guided us through all the proper production techniques and scheduling as we have grown. Thank you very much to everyone there.

BARS, BREWERIES, AND RESTAURANTS

A massive thank you to all of the bars, breweries, and restaurants across the province who carry our product and those who so generously sent in their fantastic recipes. We are honoured that you've used our spirits in so many outstanding cocktails.

THE PEOPLE AND THE PROVINCE

The Province of Newfoundland and Labrador in all of its guises has been absolutely key and integral to our development. The help of the Town

Council of Clarke's Beach, and the assistance of the Provincial Government with all the necessary permissions and advice. Thank you.

Most of all, thank you to all of the Newfoundlanders and Labradorians and "Come from Aways" who have bought our spirits since the beginning. And thank you to everyone for reading this and for sharing in our love of the perfect cocktail.

TO MY FRIENDS

You know who you are; thank you. It's been fun so far! Shall we have another round?

MY FAMILY

A huge thank you to my mother, father, and sister, for their love and support and for unstintingly encouraging me. And thank you to my immediate family for the joy and happiness they bring—especially Michelle, who has continuously aided and abetted me in the quest for the perfect cocktail (or glass of beer or wine) and, possibly more importantly, everything else in life. And to our daughters, Zoë, Xanthe, Phoebe, and Amara, who bring delight and sense to the world, make it an infinitely superior place, and seem to have inherited the ability to make a fantastic cocktail.